# BEING WITH DYING

# BEING WITH DYING

CULTIVATING COMPASSION AND FEARLESSNESS
IN THE PRESENCE OF DEATH

## Joan Halifax

*Foreword by Ira Byock, MD*

SHAMBHALA
BOSTON
2008

Shambhala Publications, Inc.
Horticultural Hall
300 Massachusetts Avenue
Boston, Massachusetts 02115
www.shambhala.com

9 8 7 6 5 4 3 2 1
First Edition
Printed in the United States of America

⊗This edition is printed on acid-free paper that meets the
American National Standards Institute z39.48 Standard.

Distributed in the United States by Random House, Inc.,
and in Canada by Random House of Canada Ltd

Designed by Gopa & Ted2, Inc.

Library of Congress Cataloging-in-Publication Data

Halifax, Joan.
Being with dying: cultivating compassion and fearlessness in the
presence of death / Joan Halifax; foreword by Ira Byock.
p. cm.
ISBN 978-1-57062-469-8 (hardcover: alk. paper)
1. Terminal care. 2. Death—Psychological aspects. I. Title.

R726.8.H35 2008
616'.029—dc22
2007042003

To Francisco Varela
(1946–2001)

"In death, you are going to be
what your experience is."

# Contents

# Foreword

BEING WITH DYING" is a phrase that aptly describes the human condition. We may be unique among species in being aware of our
mortality. Although the capacity to contemplate death is an essential human trait, most people actively eschew thinking about how their
life might end.

While the dominant orientation of Western culture toward death is
avoidance, for over 2,500 years Buddhists have studied the question of
how one can best live in the presence of death. In a sense, a life-threatening injury or disease makes Buddhists of us all, waking us from the illusion
of immortality, suddenly and from that time forth. From the moment of
diagnosis, death becomes the bell that won't stop ringing. Like a dreaded
phone call, we can try to avoid it, but the noise is always there. We can
distract ourselves with medical information and frenetic activity. We can
drink or take drugs to muffle the peal, but at quiet moments we can always
hear its ring. Ultimately, usually reluctantly, we find that only by answer-
ing the call can we hope to silence the shrill bell within.

Life-threatening illness calls us to a place—metaphorically a desert or
mountain peak—where, as we sit, the hard wind of reality strips away
all the trappings of life, like so much clothing, makeup, and accessories.
We are left naked, only "me" with my in-breath and out-breath in this
moment, here and now. Illness reveals that at every moment of every day

we are—and have always been—merely a heartbeat away from death. This incontrovertible fact need not be depressing. Instead, as Roshi Joan Halifax eloquently conveys in this remarkable book, our readiness to die can inform and enliven how we live and how we relate to one another.

Sitting with just our breath, we may find that in losing all that we have associated with life, we discover anew life within us—raw, elemental, and pure. It is not easy. The disruptions of illness can be terrifying. Guidance is welcome from someone like Roshi Joan, who is familiar with this foreboding terrain. Yet even alone, we have the wisdom of our bodies. Our inbreath provides, literally, inspiration, while the out-breath, like the sound of "Aahhhhhh," allows us to settle calmly in this new reality.

Indeed, mortality teaches us a lot about life, if we let it. People I have met as patients have often told me that having a serious, life-threatening condition forced them—or gave them the opportunity—to reprioritize the things to which they accord time and energy. Ask a person who is on a heart or liver transplant list, or someone facing cancer chemotherapy for the third or fourth time, "What matters most?" and the answer will always include the names of people they love. After the diagnosis, many people decide to swiftly complete projects or turn over work-related responsibilities to others. Most decide to spend more time with family and friends. It is common for people to place higher emphasis on aesthetic aspects of life, including food (when they can enjoy it), nature, children, music, art, and other things of beauty.

It would be wrong to give the impression that in acknowledging mortality and the approach of death, people must embrace death or become passive while preparing to "go gently into that good night." In fact, in my experience, an element of defiance often exists within an emotionally and psychologically robust attitude toward death and life. Perhaps the most defiant act in the face of death is the love of one person for another. The love of two people is a deliberate act of creation and an affirmation of life. In the context of progressive, incurable illness, love is a declaration to the force majeure that whatever else we can or cannot change, including death itself, we matter to one another!

Time and again, I have witnessed remarkable people respond to what they felt was the utter unfairness and unacceptability of death's approach by becoming ever-more-fully alive in each moment. This was not denial, but a sophisticated response to an unwanted, difficult situation. One such person, a teenage girl with recurrent leukemia, said of her waning life, "It is what it is." She knew that she had a limited time to live, yet she was not about to give death more power than it was due. Instead, she was determined to embrace life with increased intensity in whatever time she had left.

Being with dying is not a philosophical or metaphysical matter detached from the reality of life; it is rather a practice of profound and pragmatic significance. This book is a gift of wisdom and practical guidance for living.

Ira Byock, MD

# Introduction

*Healing the Divide*

IN MANY spiritual teachings, the great divide between life and death collapses into an integrated energy that cannot be fragmented. In this view, to deny death is to deny life. Old age, sickness, and death do not have to be equated with suffering; we can live and practice in such a way that dying is a natural rite of passage, a completion of our life, and even the ultimate in liberation.

The beautiful, difficult work of offering spiritual care to dying people has arisen in response to the fear-bound American version of "the good death"—a death that is too often life-denying, antiseptic, drugged-up, tube-entangled, institutionalized. And our glaring absence of meaningful ritual, manuals, and materials for a conscious death has generated a plethora of literature. Although techniques for compassionate care have been developed specifically for dying people and caregivers, many of these teachings on death can address healthy adventurers as well—acolytes eager not only to explore the full range of life's possibilities but also to focus pragmatically on the one and only certainty of our lives.

After four decades of sitting with dying people and their caregivers, I believe that studying the process of how to die well benefits even those of us who may have many years of life ahead. Of course, people who are sick or suffering, dying of old age or catastrophic illnesses, may be more receptive to exploring the great matter of dying than those who are young and healthy, or who still believe in their own indestructibility. Yet the sooner we can embrace death, the more time we have to live completely, and to live in reality. Our acceptance of our death influences not only the experience of dying but also the experience of living; life and death lie along the same continuum. One cannot—as so many of us try to do—lead life fully *and* struggle to keep the inevitable at bay.

In our discomfort, we often joke about death, the only thing as certain as taxes. Woody Allen has famously typified the attitude most of us find amusing and normal: "It's not that I'm afraid to die, I just don't want to be there when it happens."* Funny, yes; but the tragic distortion is that when you avoid death, you also avoid life. And I don't know about you, but I want to be there through all of it.

When a group of people gathers together for a meditation retreat, important shifts in one's mind and life may unfold. I often think of one retreat in particular, because what happened one day illustrates with fierce clarity the fragility of these human bodies we inhabit, and the gravity of what Buddhists call "the great matter of life and death."

This particular retreat took place sometime in the seventies at a quiet center on Cortez Island in Canada, a place then called Cold Mountain Institute. It was the beginning morning of the program, and we had just finished the first period of silent sitting meditation. The bell rang softly to announce the end of the period, and we all stretched our legs and stood up to do walking practice—but one man remained seated.

I remember feeling concern as I turned to look at him: why was he not getting up? He was still sitting in full-lotus position, his legs perfectly folded and his feet resting on his thighs. Then, as I watched in shock, his body tilted over to one side, slumped and sagging, and he fell to the floor. He died on the spot. There were several doctors and nurses participating in the retreat who helped perform CPR and administer oxygen, but

---

* From "Death: A Play" in *Without Feathers,* by Woody Allen (New York: Random House, 1975), 106.

it was too late. Later we learned that his aorta had burst while we were all sitting.

This man was healthy enough—perhaps in his late thirties. He almost certainly had not imagined when he came to this retreat that he would die during it. And yet, that day, sixty people sat down to meditate—and only fifty-nine stood up.

It's an unnerving story to most of us, who move through our lives feeling and acting as though we are immortal. We glibly reel off truisms about death being a part of life, a natural phase of the cycle of existence—and yet this is not the place from which most of us really function. Denial of death runs rampant through our culture, leaving us woefully unprepared when it is our time to die, or our time to help others die. We often aren't available for those who need us, paralyzed as we are by anxiety and resistance—nor are we available for ourselves.

As someone who works with dying people, I used to feel a little apologetic about being Buddhist, concerned that my practice might seem sectarian and inappropriate. But over the years I've seen how much the teachings of the Buddha have helped the living and the dying of every faith, and my reservations have dissolved. It's crucial that we Westerners discover a vision of death that valorizes life. The encounter between East and West has unwrapped the gifts of love and death, and now we can see that they are two sides of the coin of life. I hope this book, which reflects the forty years of work I've done in the field of care of the dying, reflects back to you some of the extraordinary possibilities that can open for each of us in life as we encounter death.

What's written here is not theoretical but grounded in my work with dying people and in the many years I have had the privilege of teaching professional and family caregivers. It is also influenced by my friendship with Roshi Bernie Glassman, who articulated the "Three Tenets," a basis for peacemaking. The Three Tenets are not-knowing, bearing witness, and compassionate action. These three reflect the kind of experiences I have had with dying people, those who are grieving, and caregivers. The tenets have become guidelines for me as I practice being with dying.

The first tenet, not-knowing, invites us to give up fixed ideas about others and ourselves and to open the spontaneous mind of the beginner. The second tenet, bearing witness, calls us to be present with the suffering and joy in the world, as it is, without judgment or any attachment to outcome. The third tenet, compassionate action, calls us to turn or return to the world with the commitment to free others and ourselves from suffering. I have used the three tenets in my work with dying since Roshi Bernie shared them with me years ago, and they are used in this book as a way for us to consider how we can be with living and dying.

As you will see, I have not made much distinction in this book between living and dying. We normally make a false dichotomy between living and dying, when in reality there is no separation between them, only interpenetration and unity. The meditations and practices offered here can be, with a few minor changes, done for oneself if ill or dying, for one's dying loved one, for oneself if one is a caregiver, for all beings, or simply because they make our living more vivid and tender.

After each chapter in this book I offer suggestions for meditations you can do on your own, so that you can have some practical experience of what it is like to begin looking at the great matter in this integrated, concentrated way. These practices are *upaya,* translated from Sanskrit as "skillful means"—the techniques and technologies we can use to be more skillful and effective in our living and our dying through training our heart and mind. They are gateways to be entered again and again, until you make them your own through your own experience with them.

I sometimes say that our monastery in Santa Fe should have a slogan hanging over the gate: "Show up." That's all we have to do when we meditate—just show up. We bring ourselves and all of our thoughts and feelings to the practice of being with whatever is, whether we are tired, angry, fearful, grieving, or just plain resistant and unwilling. It really doesn't matter what we're feeling; we just come to the temple and sit down. So experiment with using whatever arises for you as a component of your meditation practice: "Oh, look who's here today—resistance. How interesting." Or maybe: "Today I feel scared. Let's sit with that."

Our attitude of openness and inclusiveness is essential as a basis for working with dying, death, caring, and grieving. The only way to develop openness to situations as they are is by practicing the partners of presence and acceptance. We give our best to experience everything as totally as we can, not withdrawing from the vividness of any experience, no matter how scary it seems initially.

This is actually a totally ordinary state. I call it "no-big-deal dharma"— simply everyday life. It is nothing special. With this kind of open and spacious awareness, we are complete, and this moment is complete. There is nothing special to realize, no transcendent reality to achieve, nothing outside of what is unfolding in any given moment.

Contemplative practice is a completely natural activity. We can live in this straightforward way with things just as they are. Although it certainly helps to have become trained in this process through sitting meditation, we need not reserve a particular time or place, or produce a special state of mind, in order to do it. Nor do we have to force the experience on ourselves. When self-conscious effort or unusual mental experiences arise, simply observe, accept, and let them go. Notice, relax, and let go—three key aspects of mindfulness. The mind of not-knowing is simple, straightforward, open, and fresh. This kind of mind is like clouds in the sky, water flowing, a light wind; nothing obstructs it.

Whether you are thinking, writing, walking, or sitting in silence, be willing to use all of the ingredients of your life as they present themselves to you. I promise you that, as the poet Rilke wrote, "No feeling is final."*

However unbearable any discomfort seems, ultimately everything we experience is temporary. And please make the wonderful effort to show up for your life, every moment, *this* moment—because it is perfect, just as it is.

---

* Rainer Maria Rilke. "God Speaks" in *Rilke's Book of Hours: Love Poems to God,* trans. Anita Barrows and Joanna Macy (New York: Riverhead Books, 1996), 88. Used with permission.

# PART ONE

## Uncharted Territory

FOR MANY of us, the journey into being with dying begins with a diagnosis, either our own or that of a friend or relative: Alzheimer's, cancer, diabetes, a failing heart. For others, it is the loss of a son in a war, the shooting of a daughter in a school yard, the death of a coal miner under the press of earth and stone. Suddenly we're thrust into uncharted territory; we leave behind everything familiar and move into the unknown. In Buddhist terms, we're called into a realm of "not-knowing" or "beginner's mind."

In being with dying, we will encounter this not-knowing no matter how we try to map everything out or control it. We wonder, What will it feel like to die? Will I suffer? Will I be alone? Where will I go after death? Will I be missed? Is death painful? Is it a relief? In asking these questions our not-knowing is born, because in truth we cannot ever answer them.

The first tenet, not-knowing, may seem strange to us. Conceptual knowledge is so valued in our world. Yet in many cultures wisdom is equated not with knowledge but with an open heart. And how can we know what will happen in the next moment anyway? Anthropologist Arnold van Gennep calls this process of stepping away from the predictable and habitual "separation," the first phase in a rite of passage, during which we enter into the unfamiliar.* This initial phase of separation is where the mind of not-knowing is opened and affirmed. This willingness to stay open in the midst of uncertainty is what the ancient Buddhist poem "Song of the Jewel Mirror Awareness" refers to as "embracing the road."†

Wisdom, said one Zen teacher, is a ready mind. This fresh and open mind is the mind that does not rely on facts or knowledge or concepts. It is deeper than our conditioning. It is the mind that is not attached to fixed ideas about self or others. This is the courageous mind that is able to separate from the familiar landscape of mental busyness and dwell in the still reality of how things are, rather than how we think they should be. Not-knowing reflects the potential that all beings have for a clear and open mind—the wisdom mind of enlightenment that is at once groundless, intimate, transparent, inconceivable, and pervasive.

The true nature of our mind is like a great ocean, boundless, complete, and natural just as it is. Most of us choose to live on a small island in the middle of this ocean in order to feel safe and have a familiar reference point. Then we forget to look beyond our stable, seemingly secure landscape to the vastness that is who we really are.

When we die, the lines that hold us to the shore of life are cast off. We move into unknown waters, far beyond our familiar ground. André Gide reminds us that we cannot discover new lands without losing sight of the shore for a long time.‡ This is the nature of dying: letting go into the unknown, casting off our moorings, and opening to the vastness of who we really are.

---

* Arnold van Gennep, *The Rites of Passage,* trans. Monika Vizedom and Gabrielle Leboeuf Caffee (London: Routledge and Kegan Paul, 1960).
† Dongshan Laingje, "Song of the Jewel Mirror Awareness," trans. Joan Halifax and Kazuaki Tanahashi, Upaya Zen Center.
‡ André Gide, *The Counterfeiters,* trans. Dorothy Bussy (New York: Vintage Books, 1973), 353.

# 1

## A Path of Discovery
### *The Lucky Dark*

I GREW UP in the South, and one of the people I was closest to as a girl was my grandmother. I loved spending summers with her in Savannah, where she worked as a sculptor and artist, carving tombstones for local people. She was a remarkable village woman who often served her community as someone comfortable around illness and death, someone who would sit with dying friends.

And yet when she herself became ill, her own family could not offer her the same compassionate presence. My parents were good people, but like others of their social class at the time, they had no preparation for being with her as she experienced her final days. When my grandmother suffered first from cancer and then had a stroke, she was put into a nursing home and then left largely alone. And her death was long and hard.

This was in the early sixties, when the medical establishment treated dying, like giving birth, as an illness. Death was usually "handled" in a clinical setting outside the home. I visited my grandmother in a plain and cavernous room in the nursing home, a room filled with beds of people who had all been unwittingly abandoned by their kin—and I can never forget hearing her beg my father to let her die, to help her die. She needed us to be present for her, and we withdrew in the face of her suffering.

When she finally died, I felt deep ambivalence, sorrow, and relief. I looked into her coffin in the funeral home and saw that the terrible frustration that had marked her features was now gone. She seemed at last at peace. As I stood looking at her gentle face, I realized how much of her misery had been rooted in her family's fear of death, including my own. At that moment, I made the commitment to practice being there for others as they died.

Although I had been raised as a Protestant, I turned to Buddhism not long after my grandmother's death. Its teachings put my youthful suffering into perspective, and the message of the Buddha was clear and direct—freedom from suffering lies within suffering itself, and it is up to each individual to find his or her own way. But Buddhism also suggests a path through our alienation and toward freedom. The Buddha taught that we should practice helping others while cultivating deep concentration, compassion, and wisdom. He further taught that enlightenment is not a mystical, transcendent experience but an ongoing process, calling for three fundamental qualities: fearlessness, intimacy, and transparency; and that suffering diminishes when confusion and fear change into openness and strength.

In my twenties, I entered "the cave of the blue dragon," the dark space inside where the bilge of my short life had accumulated.* I knew instinctively that I had to realize healing directly through my own experience, that my habitual relationship to anguish could be resolved only by facing it fully. I felt that befriending the night was an assignment for survival, and knew intuitively that thinking about it would not be of much help. I had to *practice* with it—that is, I had to sit still and look within for my natural wisdom to show itself.

I also understood through the civil rights movement and protesting the Vietnam War that the rest of the world suffers as well. My bones told me that Buddhist teachings and practices might be the basis for working with and transforming the experience of alienation, both personal and social, so a commitment to social action began to grow strong roots inside me. I

* John Daido Loori, *Mountain Record of Zen Talks* (Boston: Shambhala Publications, 1988), 21.

found I could put my own difficulties into perspective through working with those whose problems were more difficult than mine.

My grandmother's death guided me into practicing medical anthropology in a big urban hospital in Dade County, Florida. Dying became a teacher for me, as I witnessed again and again how spiritual and psychological issues leap into sharp focus for those facing death. I discovered caregiving as a path, and as a school for unlearning the patterns of resistance so embedded in me and in my culture. Giving care, I learned, also enjoins us to be still, let go, listen, and be open to the unknown.

One thing that continually concerned me was the marginalization of people who were dying, the fear and loneliness that dying people experienced, and the shame and guilt that touched physicians, nurses, dying people, and families as the waves of death overtook life. I sensed that spiritual care could reduce fear, stress, the need for certain medications and expensive interventions, lawsuits, and the time doctors and nurses must spend reassuring people, as well as benefit professional and family caregivers, helping them to come to terms with suffering, death, loss, grief, and meaning.

As I worked with dying people, caregivers, and others experiencing catastrophe, I practiced meditation to give my life a strong spine of practice, and an open heart from which I could see beyond what I thought I knew. I was grateful to find that Buddhism offers many practices and insights for working skillfully and compassionately with suffering, pain, dying, failure, loss, and grief—the stuff of what St. John of the Cross has called "the lucky dark."* That great Christian saint recognized that suffering can be fortunate because, without it, there is no possibility for maturation. For years the lucky dark has been the atmosphere that lends clarity to my life, a life that had seen death as an enemy, but was to discover death as a teacher and guide.

As a young anthropologist, I further explored death through studying the archeological record of human history. Through the millennia and

---

* San Juan de la Cruz, "The Dark Night," in *The Poems of St. John of the Cross,* trans. John Frederick Nims (Chicago: University of Chicago Press, 1979), 19.

across cultures, the fact of death has evoked fear and transcendence, practicality and spirituality. Neolithic gravesites and the cave paintings of Paleolithic peoples capture the mystery through bones, stones, bodies curled like fetuses, and images of death and trance on cave walls.

Even today, whether people live close to the earth or in high-rise apartments, death is a deep spring. For many of us, this spring has been parched of its mystery. And yet we have an intuition that a fragment of eternity within us is liberated at the time of death. This intuition calls us to bear witness—to apprehend a part of ourselves, which has perhaps been hidden and silent.

As death draws near, a dying person may hear a still small voice inviting her to freedom. Sitting with the dying, sitting still in meditation, and sitting at the edge of cultures different from my own, I have also encountered that still small voice. It is there to speak to us all, if we can give it enough silence to be heard.

## MEDITATION

### How Do You Want to Die?

A few years ago, a dying friend read me some lines from the Hindu epic the *Mahabharata*. They made me smile. Virtuous King Yudhistara (the son of Yama, the Lord of Death) is asked, "What is the most wondrous thing in the world?" And Yudhistara replies, "The most wondrous thing in the world is that all around us people can be dying and we don't believe it can happen to us."*

In teaching care of the dying, I often begin by asking questions that explore our stories around death, including the legacies we may have inherited from culture and family. Looking at our stories may help us be taught by what we believe will happen when we are dying, and open new possibilities for us.

---

* Jane Polden, *Regeneration: Journey through the Mid-Life Crisis* (New York: Continuum, 2002).

We begin with a very direct and plain question: "What is your worst-case scenario of how you will die?" The answer to this question lurks underneath the skin of our lives, subconsciously shaping many of the choices we make about how we lead them. In this powerful practice of self-inquiry, I ask you to write it all down, freely and in detail (telling how, when, of what, with whom, and where), about the worst death you can imagine for yourself. Write from your most uncensored, uncorrected state of mind, and let all the unprescribed elements of your psyche emerge as you write. Take about five minutes for this.

When you are finished, ask yourself how you feel, how your body feels, and what is coming up for you—and write down these responses as well. It is crucial at this point to practice honest self-observation. What is your body telling you? Give yourself a few minutes to write down how imagining this worst-case death makes you feel.

Then take another five minutes to answer a second question: "How do you really want to die?" Again, please write about this in as much detail as possible. What is your ideal time, place, and kind of death? Who will be there with you? And a second time, when you have finished, give some attention to what is happening in your body and mind, writing these reflections down as well.

If you can, do this exercise with someone else, so you can see how different your answers are. Amazingly, your worst fears might well not be shared by others, and your ideas about an ideal death might not be someone else's. My own answers to these questions have changed as time has passed. Years ago, I felt that the worst death would be a lingering one. Today I feel that it would be harder to die a senseless, violent death. A lingering death might give me the time to prepare myself more fully. In addition, in my dying I might be of some use to others.

At a divinity school where I taught several classes on death and dying, one-third of the class answered that they wanted to die in their sleep. And in other settings where I have posed these questions, more people wanted to die alone and in peace than I would have guessed. Quite a few wanted to die in nature. Among the thousands of responses I have received to this question, only a few people said they wanted to die in a hospital or nursing home, although that is in fact where many of us will die. And almost everyone wanted to die in some way that was fundamentally spiritual. A violent and random death was regarded as one of the worst possibilities. Dying painlessly and with spiritual support and a sense of meaning was considered to be the best of all possible worlds.

Finally, after exploring how you want to die, ask yourself a third question: "What are you willing to do to die the way you want to die?" We go through a lot to educate and train ourselves for a vocation; most of us invest a great deal of time in taking care of our bodies, and we usually devote energy to caring for our relationships. So now please ask yourself what you are doing to prepare for the possibility of a sane and gentle death. And how can you open up the possibility for the experience of deathless enlightenment both at this moment and when you die?

# 2

## The Heart of Meditation
### *Language and Silence*

Y EARS AGO I spent time with an old Tibetan lama who seemed to be rejoicing as his death approached. I asked him whether he was happy because he was old and ready to die. He replied that he felt like a child who was returning to his mother. All his life had been a preparation for death. He told me that his long preparation for death had actually given him his life. Now that he was about to die, he would finally open his mind to its true nature.

A spiritual practice can give us a refuge, a shelter in which to develop insight about what is happening both outside us and within our minds and hearts. It can provide stability, which is just as important for caregivers as it is for those of us actively dying. It can cultivate wholesome mental qualities, such as compassion, joy, and nonattachment—qualities that give us the resilience to face and possibly transform suffering. And a spiritual practice can be a place where what Keats called the "negative capability" of uncertainty and doubt can transform into a refuge of truth.

One dying woman described her experience of meditation as being held in the arms of her mother. She said she wasn't escaping from her suffering when meditating, but rather she felt met by kindness and strength. As she let go into her pain and uncertainty, she realized the truth of not-knowing in that very surrender. This experience gave her much greater equanimity.

Our own feelings can be powerful and disturbing as we sit quietly with a dying person, bear witness to the emotional outpouring of grieving relatives, or struggle to be fully present and stable as we face the fear and anger, sadness and confusion, of those whose lives are going through radical change. We may want to find ways to accept and transform the heat or cold of our own mental states. If we have established a foundation in a contemplative discipline, then we may find stillness, spaciousness, and resilience in the storm—even in the storm of our own difficulties around dying.

Buddhists often refer to their regular schedule of meditation as a practice—because we are practicing being present. We don't have to get it perfect, we just have to show up for it. And a regular meditation practice offers us the sister gifts of language and silence, gifts that often come arm in arm to help. Language brings crucial insights into our minds and hearts, while silence is integral for cultivating that deep concentration, tranquillity, and mental stability within us. Contemplative strategies using these sister gifts prepare us both for dying and for caregiving. Some involve silence, focus, and openness, while others involve nurturing a positively oriented imagination or generating wholesome mental qualities.

Often we feel that silence and stillness aren't good enough when suffering is present. We feel compelled to "do something"—to talk, console, work, clean, move around, "help." But in the shared embrace of meditation, a caregiver and dying person can be held in an intimate silence beyond consolation or assistance. When sitting with a dying person, I try to ask myself carefully, What words will benefit her? Does anything really need to be said? Can I know greater intimacy with her through a mutuality beyond words and actions? Can I relax and trust in simply being here, without needing my personality to mediate the tender connection we share?

One dying man told me, "I remember being with my mother as she was dying. She was old like I am now and was ready to go. I used to just sit with her, hold her hand. . . . Will you hold mine?" So we sat together in silence, with touch joining our hearts.

Like silence, words can truly be of service. We may rely on the gift of language—whether prayer, poetry, dialogue, or guided meditation—as a way to reveal the meaning in moments and things. Listening to the testimony of a dying person or a grieving family member can serve the one speaking; it all depends on *how* we listen. Maybe we can reflect back the words and feelings in such a way that the speaker can at last really hear what he's said. And bearing witness like this also gives us as listeners insight and inspiration. Language can loosen the knot that has tied a person to the hard edge of fear and bring this person home to compassionate, heart-opening truths. Good words or a guided meditation can also cultivate a positive attitude and skillful means for attending to the issues.

Mindfulness, the core of everything that we do in being with dying, is a practice of giving deep attention to what is happening in the present moment—what is happening in the mind and body of the observer and also what is going on in our surroundings. We might practice being mindful of the body, the breath, or the experience of physical change (including sickness and pain). We can also experience being mindful of our responses—the feelings that arise in reaction to pleasure or discomfort—and watching them arise and disappear. And finally we can study our mental states—such as longing, anger, confusion, concentration, clarity, or feeling scattered. These are the four foundations of mindfulness: the body, feeling, the mind, and the objects of mind.

Trust and patience combined with openness and acceptance—qualities nurtured by mindfulness practice—enable us to sustain ourselves in being with dying. These qualities help us develop the necessary relationship between compassion and equanimity and learn to respond from a place that is deeper than our personality and our conceptual mind. With equanimity and compassion as inseparable companions in our work we are also less judgmental and less attached to outcomes. For me, mindfulness practice has been the ground of my learning and practice of caregiving. It has given many of us access to the still inner space from which we must learn to draw our strength and wisdom.

Mindfulness practice also helps us stabilize the mind and the body. It helps us be less reactive, more responsive and more resilient. It reduces stress and opens our intuitive capacities.

Mindfulness is energized by the aspiration to help others. A commitment based in an altruistic state of mind helps us to break from our strong self-attachment. The desire to serve also helps to give our practice energy and depth and makes it more tender and inclusive.

Whether praying or meditating, we need to bring our whole being to our meditation practice if the practice is going to have real benefit. Our intention to practice in order to help others and the commitment, wholeheartedness, and energy we bring to our practice make a big difference in the quality and outcome of our meditation. When we fall in love, for example, we put a lot of energy into bringing our very best to our beloved. If we are told we are gravely ill, we will try hard to find a cure. Our spiritual practice requires the same degree of commitment and effort.

We should also be aware that unrealistic expectations can be a problem. A meditation practice is not a quick fix for long-standing mental habits that are causing suffering. Just as the body needs to be slowly stretched for greater flexibility, so does the mind need time for its training. We can't lift heavy weights in a day if we have not conditioned the body to do so. We can't immediately go to a high altitude if the body isn't ready. If our expectations are too great and we start having trouble, we might well abandon our practice.

In fact, so-called trouble should be expected, because when we stop our habitual mental and physical activity and sit quietly, difficulties often become more visible. We can become even more sensitive to suffering and feel at risk for a breakdown. What is probably breaking down is the ego—our identity as a small, separate self—and the healthy part of us should welcome this. But often, accepting the raw and difficult feelings that accompany the deconstruction of the ego may not be that easy. Be patient, and know that all of the meditative techniques in this book have been developed over years of trial and error. And time is needed for them to be effective, so be patient. Difficulties with your practice might even be indicative that your practice is working. Even if patience or letting go aren't easy for you, try to suspend judgment and gently remind yourself of these qualities whenever resistance is present. We have to be willing to risk everything, especially the things we most want to clutch to ourselves.

Finally, don't forget the importance of commitment, consistency, and motivation, all of which take effort. We can't just sit there and expect something magical to happen. Bring all of yourself to your meditation, including the heart of acceptance when it seems as if there is no reason to carry on. Accept this feeling and then go forward. When these very resistances are used to support our meditation practice, they give it strength and depth—the very same qualities of mind that make our encounter with dying more sane.

Alongside effort, cultivate awareness whenever you aren't actually meditating, staying in touch with the present moment. Whatever we do in this work with dying people, we vow to do it mindfully, whether giving a sponge bath, changing a bedpan, sitting silently with a sick friend, sitting in silence with ourselves. Formal mindfulness practice gives us a spacious and powerful container in which to cultivate this awareness—and we need that kind of concentration, because in being with dying, our mindfulness will be routinely challenged by all kinds of complex conditions: working with families in extreme states of grief, rage, or frustration; working with dying people suffering almost unbearable pain, fear, denial, or isolation; sitting with a friend who is caught in the slow tide of Alzheimer's, or a mother whose son has been murdered. Concentrated awareness synchronizes body, speech, and mind, bringing our full attention to the immediate situation without adding anything extra.

When we are learning to practice mindfulness—and even when we have been meditating for many years—we bring our concentration to that most intimate object, our breath. We abide in that intimacy. We then expand our concentration to include our body, learning to dwell in the oneness of breath, mind, and body. Once we are familiar with this state, we can open our concentration to include the world around us. Slowly we expand our confidence beyond the razor-topped fences of our fear. This is how we can come into an unbroken, intimate relationship with existence itself.

## Meditation

### *Strong Back, Soft Front*

The practice of following the breath and stilling the mind is not only central to Buddhist practice, I believe it is crucial for the practice of being with dying as well. In this meditation, we'll learn how to settle down and find stillness inside ourselves, helping us be at peace with every moment, no matter what that moment brings.

Sit down, in a comfortable position where you will be able to hold still for some time, whether in a chair or on a meditation cushion. After you sit down, slowly become aware of your breath and your body. Let your body soften. If you are sitting on a chair, relax your legs and put both feet flat on the floor. If you are sitting on a cushion, you can arrange your legs in whatever way is most comfortable, but be sure not to cut off the circulation. Be present to a sense of gravity. Invite the groundedness of the earth into your body and mind. Let your whole body experience the strength of your stable connection with the earth. Relax into the firmness of this stability.

Now bring your awareness into your spine. Breathe into your spine. Appreciate how vertical, strong, flexible, and conductive it is. Rock gently from side to side as you settle your posture. The strength of your spine allows you to uphold yourself in the midst of any condition. You can remind yourself of this strength by silently saying, "Strong back." Your mind and your back are connected. Feel the sense of uprightness and flexibility in your mind.

Now let your awareness go to your belly. Breathe into your belly. Let your breath be deep and strong as your belly rises and falls. Feel your natural courage and openness as you breathe deeply into your belly. Shifting your awareness to your chest, touch the tender, open feeling of this space. Let yourself be present to your own suffering and to the fact that, just like you, others also suffer. Imagine being free of suffering and helping others be free too. Feel the strength of your resolve rising up from your belly. Let your heart be open and permeable. Release any tightness as you allow your breath to pass through your heart. Remind yourself of your own tenderness by saying, "Soft front."

Now bring your awareness to your lungs. With your spine straight, let your breath fully enter your lungs. Fill your lungs softly with air. With gratitude, remember that your life is supported by each breath. At this point the whole front of your body may begin to feel open, receptive, and permeable. Through your open body, you can feel the world, which lends compassion. Through your strong spine, you can be with suffering, which gives you equanimity. Let these qualities of equanimity and compassion intermingle. Let them inform one another and give you genuine presence. *Strong back, soft front.* This is the essence of our work in being with dying.

Bringing awareness to your shoulders, let them soften and relax. Then shift your focus to your hands. Experiment with the following two hand positions and see how they inform your state of mind. One position is to rest your hands on your knees, leaving the front of your body open. This is a way of entering into shared awareness as you subtly welcome everything into your consciousness. Alternatively you can put your hands together in front of your belly, which strengthens internal awareness and concentration.

What you do with your eyes affects your mind. Your eyes can be gazing forward, not grasping onto anything. They can be slightly open, gazing down at the floor. Or they can be closed. With your eyes gazing open, you can be with life as it unfolds, bringing forth a sense of luminosity to the phenomenal world. With your eyes slightly open, you are at the threshold between your mind and the outer world. Not entering either world, you bring both together in emptiness. With your eyes closed, you relax into an undistracted concentration.

Whatever sounds, sights, smells, tastes, or feelings arise, simply let them pass in and out of your awareness as you keep your mind on your breath. Allow yourself simplicity. You are relaxing in such a way that you can begin to drop into a place that is deeper than your personality, deeper than your identity, deeper than your story.

When we have completed our meditation practice, we offer to others whatever good has arisen for us. We also remind ourselves to bring the spirit of practice into our everyday life in order to help others.

This is the basic meditation we will return to throughout the book. Following the breath for a few moments is the best way I have found to settle the mind and body and prepare for any more complicated or potentially arousing practices. I often use the breath as the object of my attention, because this very life depends on it. Furthermore, you can discover your state of mind by the quality of your breath—is it ragged or smooth, shallow or deep, fast or slow? Often you can calm yourself by regulating your breathing. Whenever things get too fraught or scattered, you can always return to the breath for as long as you need to ground yourself again.

# 3

## Overcoming the Porcupine Effect
### *Moving Past Fear into Tenderness*

WORLD RELIGIONS SCHOLAR Huston Smith once told the story of a well-known psychologist, an ornery old man close to death. One morning as he was struggling to get to the toilet, a nurse tried to help him. He snapped back at her, "I can do it myself!" Then he dropped to the floor dead.

Smith used this story to illustrate just how defensive about needing help we often are. He called this reaction "the porcupine effect." Some of us have dependency issues, and a hard time receiving support from others, thus we may repress our fundamental tenderness toward each other.

All too often our so-called strength comes from fear, not love; instead of having a strong back, many of us have a defended front shielding a weak spine. In other words, we walk around brittle and defensive, trying to conceal our lack of confidence. If we strengthen our backs, metaphorically speaking, and develop a spine that's flexible but sturdy, then we can risk having a front that's soft and open, representing choiceless compassion. The place in your body where these two meet—strong back and soft front—is the brave, tender ground in which to root our caring deeply when we begin the process of being with dying.

How can we give and accept care with strong-back, soft-front compassion, moving past fear into a place of genuine tenderness? I believe it

comes about when we can be truly transparent, seeing the world clearly—
and letting the world see into us.

Zen priest Issan Dorsey gave me a great lesson in how transparency
works. Issan founded the Hartford Street Zen Center and the Maitri AIDS
Hospice in the gay district of San Francisco. He had not been diagnosed
as HIV-positive himself, but believed it was crucial to offer help to his
brothers dying all around him. Although the building was physically very
small, anything and anybody could fit under its roof. Issan was a big-roof
Buddhist.

From time to time Issan and I led retreats together, and he eventually
invited me to be on the board of the hospice. Through Issan's work, I saw
how Buddhism could function in a practical way for a community in crisis. At the hospice you didn't feel piety. You just took refuge alongside
others, and that refuge was as big as the sky. The practice there had been
energized by the dross of suffering—not consumed by it.

One day, Issan was diagnosed with AIDS. We hoped he would live a
long time, but as it turned out, he had only a few short years left inside
him. Shortly before his death, Issan received dharma transmission from
his teacher, Richard Baker Roshi. Dharma transmission in Zen Buddhism
is the confirmation of a student's awakening. Issan was so frail he could
barely walk to the altar for the ceremony. Wearing a bathrobe, he rose
shakily from his chair and took a few feeble steps toward his teacher. Baker
met him halfway, and a big lotus flower bloomed at that moment.

I believe Issan had received dharma transmission many times before
that day. He was transparent to himself and to those around him. He
wasn't impeded by opinions, identities, or concepts. After one of Issan's
talks, a friend said to me, "How wonderful—not a single idea!"

Issan's health continued to decline. One day I came up from Southern
California to visit him in the hospital. Although I have been at the bedside
of many dying people, watching Issan die was hard for me. He had been
there for so many. He was a good friend, a role model, and also lots of fun.
His life taught us all what it meant to be a true human being, present for
another in such a way that any sense of "other" disappeared. Sometimes
that disappearing was in laughter; sometimes it was in silence. Sometimes

he looked with his brown eyes right into the heart of the matter. Like so many others, I wanted my friend to continue to live.

Thin and fragile, wrapped in a hospital gown, Issan was sitting up in bed in the late afternoon when I went to visit him, maybe a month before he died. I sat on the side of his bed, and suddenly my face was wet with tears. Issan reached over to touch my hand. He looked at me and said, "It is not necessary." Then he smiled.

In that gesture of kindness, something I had not seen before became clear to me. I thought that I had come there to care for Issan, but in fact Issan was caring for me. Like a true Buddha of pure, unmediated compassion, he had held up a mirror allowing me to see through my unnecessary pity, which was extra, and to see into the truth of our friendship. Something subtle—beyond pity, beyond language—connected the two of us and made us transparent to each other. We cannot realize this kind of liberation without the presence of relatedness. This is where spirit appears—not in an individual but between individuals. When this happens, the distinction between self and other simply vanishes, as the spines of fear disappear from around the heart. In that moment of transparent communion, Issan and I seemed to have opened the treasure box of love and death.

How can we develop this transparency? I think about it sometimes in terms of a lotus flower. The roots of the pure white lotus are buried deep in the pond's dark mud. But it's that very mud that nurtures and feeds the lotus, making it possible for the flower to open in splendor to the sun.

The lotus flower is really our awakened mind, nourished by suffering. Maybe some of us have been hiding in the cast-off and rotting selves of our past that lie at the bottom of the heart. Now we are asked to use our suffering as food and fuel, to make our lives and the life of the world more visible. It's time to consume the wet, dank stuff of suffering that has made our life so heavy and hard to deal with. In our practice, we become bottom-feeders, eating lotus-food so that we have the strength to open up our hearts and minds to the world, the way Issan did.

Often it takes an accident, a catastrophic diagnosis, or a disaster for us to break open and be able to accept our own suffering in a bigger, more patient way. But suffering also makes us tender. When we are very sensitive, we may want to protect ourselves through withdrawing. Suffering is a sword that can cut both ways—it can free us or send us into hiding.

To meet suffering and bear witness to it without collapsing or withdrawing into alienation, first we must stabilize the mind and make friends with it. Next, we open the mind to life—the whole of life, within and around us, seeing it clearly and unconditionally from that stable inner base. And then we fearlessly open our hearts to the world, welcoming it inside no matter how wretched or full of pain it might be. I've come to call this the "threefold transparency"—us being transparent to ourselves, the world's being transparent to us, and us being transparent to the world.

It helps to approach each person, each situation, with a sense of openness, a mind of not-knowing. Often this is difficult; we mistakenly think that our practical caregiving skills are all we have to give. Yet our presence born of openness is really the greatest offering we can make. Even as we are doing for another, our being supports that doing. It is how we can best bear witness. An older man who worked with hospice once told me, "I try to leave everything I know in the car before I go into the house of someone who is dying." Pretending we "know" just covers up our fear.

No matter how busy we are, we can bring simple contemplative elements into our caregiving practice that will help us to follow the dying person's lead and to give no fear. Sharing practice or prayer, silence and presence, with a dying person also serves the caregiver's well-being. When you find yourself caught up in the events around you or in your own hope and fear, slow down. Even stop. Cultivate the habit of attending to the breath continually; use the breath to stabilize and concentrate the mind.

We can also use words to generate a state of presence and self-compassion. For example, the following reminders can be helpful. I use them in my own practice, and share them with other caregivers and dying people. On the inhalation, say to yourself, "Breathing in, I calm body and mind." On the exhalation: "Breathing out, I let go." Inhalation: "Dwelling in the present moment." Exhalation: "This is the only moment." I learned a version of this from the Buddhist teacher Thich Nhat Hanh many years ago. It has been a good friend since.

Another way to connect to the moment is to use the sense fields. Look out the window at the sky for a moment. Listen attentively to the sounds in the room. Touch the dying person mindfully. Take a few sips of cool water. Be fully with a detail in the present moment. Then breathe deeply and relax the tension in your body as you exhale. Remember why you are doing this work.

Tibetan Buddhists say that we have all been one another's mother in a previous lifetime. Imagining every being as your mother, practice offering love equally to all whom you encounter, including strangers, creatures, and even those who have hurt you. This practice isn't always easy for some of us Westerners, who may have conflicted relationships with our mothers. But I can imagine a being who has given me and others life, protection, nourishment, and kindness. When I'm giving care to a dying person, I try both to give and receive kindness as if I were the dying one's mother and to see the dying one as my mother, saying silently to myself, "Now it is time for me to repay the great kindness of all motherly beings." Thinking of all beings with motherly love is a good reference point when I have fallen into automatic behavior, am feeling alienated, or am having trouble opening my heart.

Years ago, I visited a Buddhist nunnery located in the thick, wet jungle north of Bangkok, Thailand. Huge columnar limestone formations poked out of the forest's crown. When I drove up to the main area of the center, I was a little surprised that the *kutis,* or meditation huts, were caged in. And tied to the cages were large, bright red, stuffed toy crocodiles. It was a pretty bizarre sight.

Even more interesting were the hundreds of monkeys turning somersaults all around the place. It was a veritable zoo, but the nuns were caged in, not the monkeys.

I left my car with just a little bit of trepidation, as there were so many overly friendly monkeys. As I made my way to the main area of the nunnery, with monkeys dancing all around me, the old abbess invited me to sit down in their midst and talk about practice with her. I thought to myself, "Another interesting Buddhist experience."

Amid the chatter of hundreds of monkeys, I was assailed by a terrible odor. Not to seem impolite, I kept my eyes on my hostess as our conversation about meditation continued. Finally, I had to look around to see what was the source of this rotten smell. My eyes fell on a monkey whose eyes were filled with terrible distress. In her arms was a baby monkey who had been dead for some time. Its little body was bloated, the eyes filled with insects.

I was stunned. I could not believe what I was seeing. She reminded me of Kisagotami, who would not give up the dead body of her son. In the case of Kisagotami, the Buddha and her village helped her recognize the truth that all beings share mortality. For this mother monkey, there was no Buddha to help her see the truth of impermanence and the futility of clinging.

In the midst of the roil of monkeys all around, my eyes met the eyes of this mother monkey, and we rested in mutual sorrow for some minutes. In my heart, I begged her to let her baby go. It was time. And in that instant, some kind of intelligent look took hold of her face, she turned, and slowly walked off into the dark jungle with her baby clutched in one arm. Somehow she had been trusting enough to stop, and I had been trusting enough to meet her as well.

Our true essence is that of a buddha, a word meaning simply "awake." And really, the aim of all contemplative practice is realizing this inherent availability, this experience of being simply unselfish. The awakened state is what lies underneath our personality, history, culture, expectations, and even beyond our species. If conditions are right, anyone can awaken to the basic reality that the mind-stream is pure and the heart is good. This is why we meditate; this is why we contemplate; this is why we pray: to bring us home to who we really are. See what happens when we hold this thought in every moment: "I will free myself from entanglement, from despair, from misery, and realize one heart, one mind." Remember, awakening occurs through intimacy and transparency—look closely and see that all of us are tied to one another through bonds of suffering and also through bonds of freedom.

Please discover that transparency is the very foundation of fearlessness, and realize transparency in all three dimensions. First, become transparent to yourself through personal inquiry. Your meditation and sense of deep interiority reveal your mind, and all that it holds. Then, make the world transparent to you. See into the nature of reality, into the hearts of others, into the heart of the world. And finally, become transparent to others. Learn to be open, vulnerable, and undefended in your relationships. Realizing these three transparencies requires all of us to plunge into the unknown and unknowable of our own heart and mind and to open our heart to the world. This is the love that Issan showed me as he touched my hand and gave me no fear; this is the connection I felt with that mother monkey whose sorrow seemed to run so deep.

## MEDITATION

### Mercy—Exchanging Self with Other

Someone once told me that mercy is the grace of compassion. It is one of the ways we express our love and nonduality in relation to each other. Mercy is a quality of great value for our work with dying people and those who are suffering. How can we give care without mercy? Mercy needs to be there, or our care is cold and mechanical, defended and shrunken with fear, or tentative and distracted.

The following practice is so simple, and yet maybe one of the hardest things we can do. It is a practice of ultimate and extreme compassion, a brave act of love when we can really see through the eyes of another.

First, remember why you are practicing. Recall your aspiration, this vow to really be of benefit to others, this vow to awaken from your own suffering. Let your practice rest in the hands of your good heart as you remember your innermost request.

Now, bring to your mind and heart the presence of someone who is suffering deeply. Maybe this person is sitting before you right now.

Open your heart and mind to him. Feel your way into this person's heart. Look out through his eyes. Really imagine that you are this person, living his life, feeling his suffering, and knowing his true heart.

Be this person. Feel into how he experiences his world, his life. Exchange yourself for this person at the deepest level.

After some time has passed, let yourself rest in unconditioned presence. End the practice by dedicating the merit to the well-being of others.

# 4

## The Wooden Puppet and Iron Man
### Selfless Compassion, Radical Optimism

Over the years people have asked me questions like "How can you touch someone whose body is covered with lesions?" "Isn't it difficult to be around so much pain and suffering?" "Don't you feel worn out from giving so much?" "What kind of gratification is there in doing this kind of work when the outcome is death?" "Don't people's emotions overwhelm you?" "Isn't it frightening to be around dying all the time?" "Don't you get numb from facing loss and sorrow so often?"

In the beginning it wasn't easy. It did not come naturally or instinctively. Working so closely with death often scared me; I was afraid I might get what the dying person had. When I recognized, however, that I already have what dying people have—mortality—I stopped being afraid of catching it.

Recognizing this very interconnectedness is the ground of giving no fear, and the beginning of compassion. Patient and caregiver are one and the same, connected by life and death as by suffering and joy. When we manage to step through fear by reconnecting with each other, real compassion arises.

Zen uses the images of the iron man and the wooden puppet to describe giving no fear. The iron man—or iron woman—embodies compassion through unshakable strength and equanimity. He exemplifies the three qualities of resoluteness, resilience, and durability. He's not attached to outcome, and has absolutely no interest in offering consolation—he expresses love without pity. With his deep equanimity, the iron man works from a pivot of intention that allows him to be fully present and immovable in this very moment. He puts himself in a difficult position and is strengthened by it as he offers strength to it. This is the very heart of our work with being with dying, this ongoing practice of sublime defeat, like a tempered sword, defeated by the fire and pounded to become strong.

My father was an "iron man" as he faced his death. A friend with AIDS was an "iron man" as he lay in my arms and accepted his death as a gift to all those who suffered like him. One caregiver friend showed an "iron woman's" strength as she sat quietly by her mother's bedside, bearing witness to four days of unrelenting, wild anger that finally resolved into bliss at the moment of her mother's death.

The other Buddhist image for giving no fear is the wooden puppet, a very different kind of symbol for compassion. The puppet simply responds to the world as it is. There is no self; there is no other. Someone is hungry; food is given. Someone is thirsty; drink is offered. Someone is sleepy; a bed is made. For the wooden puppet, the world is the puppeteer to which she seamlessly responds without strategy, motivation, or thought of outcome. She can always be counted on because her front is soft and open; to be a wooden puppet is to bear witness and respond to suffering with a tenderness that knows no bounds.

The wooden puppet and the iron man both practice what I call "radical optimism." They don't have expectations about a specific outcome—about dying a good death, or being a perfect caregiver. And because they don't have these ideas or expectations, they can really practice optimism. This kind of optimism arises directly out of not-knowing. It's free of time and space, self and other—yet it's embedded in the very stuff of our daily lives.

This might sound cryptic, but it has real meaning in being with dying. When I sit with a dying person, or with prisoners in maximum security at the local penitentiary, if I allow one single thought of outcome to rear its head, the truth of the moment dies. I've stopped being with what is and I've started to have ideas about the way I think it should be.

People often ask me about having a "good death." But in the view of the radical optimist, there is no good or bad death. Being with dying is simply being with dying; each being does it his or her way. With no gaining idea, no attachment to outcome, the radically optimistic caregiver bears witness and gives no fear. An old Zen saying offers another way of putting it: "Fishing with a straight hook"—meaning, don't look for results. Whether at the beginning, in the middle, or at the end, just exist in the right-now.

A friend of mine with AIDS struggled long and hard in his dying. But he finally came to a place where, after a lot of pain, he decided that he was suffering for all men who had Kaposi's sarcoma. In this way he brought himself into peace. As he felt his connection with all those whose bodies bloomed with purple lesions, his self-absorption left him, and he was flooded with love. He told me one day that he could see why Christ's suffering was a model for ours. "When you suffer, you suffer along with everyone else," he said. In his pain, he knew he was not alone.

As he spoke, I saw a tear of relief slide slowly down his cheek. His fingers reached out to mine. There was nothing to say. We simply let our fingers touch and intertwine. He then asked me to hold him and sing. As I held him, he looked like a small, emaciated child, purple blooms covering his body. He sighed in tune with the simple song he had requested. For a time, he was completely relaxed and seemed to be free of pain. And I relaxed, too. He had given both of us a deep reason to live and to let go.

A spiritual life is not about being self-conscious, or wearing a button that says "I'm a bodhisattva!" It is about doing what you have to do with no attachment to outcome. True compassion just does what needs to be done because it's the only thing to do—just because it's natural and ordinary, like smoothing your pillow at night. Sometimes the outcome can seem to be a happy one. And often enough we are faced with so-called failure. And thus it is.

There's a famous Zen story about compassion that consists of a dialogue between two brothers, Tao Wu and Yun Yen. It goes like this:

> Yun Yen asked Tao Wu, "What does the Bodhisattva of Great Compassion use so many hands and eyes for?"
> Wu said, "It's like someone reaching back, groping for a pillow in the middle of the night."
> Yen said, "I understand."
> Wu said, "How do you understand it?"
> Yen said, "All over the body are hands and eyes."
> Wu said, "You have said quite a bit there, but you've only said eighty percent of it."
> Yen said, "What do you say, Elder Brother?"
> Wu said, "Throughout the body are hands and eyes."*

This conversation seems kind of mysterious, until we think about what a "bodhisattva" really is—a Buddhist archetype of compassion and fearlessness, an awakened being who has vowed to come back lifetime after lifetime in order to save others from suffering. Bodhisattvas could leave our world of pain and suffering behind forever, but they deliberately choose to be reborn into the terrible and beautiful wilderness of life to practice compassion. Earthly bodhisattvas are those men and women, those wooden puppets and iron men, who have dedicated their lives to awakening these qualities—whether caregivers or those receiving care. In the metaphor Yunyan uses, they're covered with eyes that see others' needs, and hands that reach out to help.

So this exchange between the two brothers teaches us that true compassion, with its myriad hands and eyes, is every bit as natural and ordinary as pulling the pillow toward your head in the darkness of night. Then Daowu goes further: he observes that compassion is like the blood in our body, like the nerves running through our fingers—it *is* our whole being.

---

* From *The Blue Cliff Record*, trans. Thomas Cleary and J. C. Cleary (Boston: Shambhala Publications, 1977), 489.

In total compassion, Daowu suggests, throughout the whole body, we feel and give no fear.

My friend Susanna, an anthropologist, lived with Huichol Indians in northwestern Mexico when she was a young woman. One day she met a large Huichol family as they visited the remote mountain village where she lived. The mother held a baby in her arms, an infant that looked ill and neglected. When Susanna asked what was wrong with the baby, the mother told her the little one was dying. Horrified, Susanna wanted to know why they weren't doing anything; but the mother simply repeated that the baby was going to die.

Bewildered by what was happening, she asked the family if they would let her take care of it. She took the little one, washed and fed her, wrapped her snugly in a thick blanket, curled up around her, and fell asleep. When she woke in the morning, the baby was dead. The parents reminded her that they already told her the child would die. As she related this incident to me twenty years later, she said very simply that she would still do nothing different.

Death is inescapable. All beings, you and me, are heading straight into its mouth. What kind of optimism can be born from such a raw truth? "Learn to cooperate with the inevitable," Jonas Salk once advised me. In the bright light of the inevitable, how do we sustain buoyancy, optimism, and the heart to help others?

Simple, but not necessarily easy: We abandon our fixed ideas of outcome. If there is even one wish for a certain kind of result, then we aren't being with what's actually happening. The radical optimist is not investing in the future, but in the present moment, free of design. Only a radical optimist can bear to bear witness. When I sit across from the man on death row who raped and killed an eleven-year-old girl, his eyes stare into mine through the food port in his narrow cell door; any thought of "saving his soul" would destroy the truth of that moment. I watch ideas about what I want for him arise, and I let them go with a breath. When I touch the hand of an old woman as the breath rattles out of her body, wanting to make her dying easier would only be an obstacle to my being there with her. Can we hold such moments without a sense of tragedy, frustration, or fear? I, for one, don't find it easy—I have a basic intolerance of suffering. But I give it my close attention, while holding myself as open as possible.

Years ago, a student of mine contracted kidney cancer while still a young man. One day as I was visiting him, he complained about his useless life of the past. Only now was he having a taste of what he thought was really important to him, a life that was not about making deals and making money, but a life that might be of help to others, a life where suffering was teaching him about humility and kindness, a life that was without hope, in the best sense of the word. In spite of pain after surgery and with an undetermined prognosis, his spirits were high and he felt an unusual optimism.

As it turned out, my friend's cancer went into remission. During this period, he was grateful beyond words for what had happened to him. He was free of cancer, and his enthusiasm for life and his love of others was like a fresh lake after rain. He valued most especially the insight that he could now live a different kind of life if he wanted to. At the same time, he also expressed concern that he might forget and fall back into his old ways.

Robert Aitken Roshi once said that he was not so interested in the day you attained enlightenment—he was interested in the day after! As my friend feared, after a year went by, he forgot his commitment to his inner life as his old priorities again took hold of him. He went about his everyday living rarely giving thought to the fact that he had recently recovered from cancer. He went back into doing business, and we saw little of each other. When we did meet, he spoke only about money and women.

Several years later, when we met again, slightly wiser for his misery, he wondered aloud what had happened. He saw that the habit of materialism was so strong in him that not even the threat of dying of cancer had been enough to keep him on the path for long. He felt that he was living a lie and denying the gift of insight that had been given to him as a result of his illness. He felt deeply dissatisfied.

Another year went by, and my friend increasingly felt that life was meaningless. He found himself in another catastrophe, but this one was psychological: he was suffering from severe depression. He felt angry with himself and at the world, and helpless in the face of his habits of mind. As

I sat with him, listening to him pour out his unhappiness and failure to find anything worthwhile in his life, I tried to let go of my expectations of a good outcome for my young friend. My only job was to bear witness to his suffering and at the same time to see his good heart steadily beating underneath all of his misery.

One day, he said to me, "You seem to see something that I don't." I asked him what it was that he thought I saw. He paused and then replied, "I think you see who I really am." I asked him what that was, and he said, "I don't know, but when you see it, I can feel it." At that moment, we both relaxed and smiled together for the first time in five years. Although he had lost sight of the gifts suffering had brought him, he regained his vision. I felt glad that I'd borne witness to both his suffering and his true nature, so that he, too, could glimpse his own fundamental goodness.

Tibetan teacher Chögyam Trungpa Rinpoche often talked about "spiritual materialism," meaning our desire to "get" enlightenment and even our noble-seeming aspirations to help others. Aspiring to awaken, or to benefit others, can be useful—it often helps with our priorities, just as having the goal of a sane and conscious death can help us to appreciate and relish this present moment. But if practice becomes a means to a "greater" end, then it becomes an investment—and we start expecting a profit. How can we be at one with a particular moment if we're expecting something? How can we die freely if we're fettered with the expectation of a so-called "good death?" And how can we really serve others if we're attached to our particular altruistic outcome? When we first start to practice, and for a long time thereafter, altruism can give our practice body and depth. The commitment engendered by kindness helps us to remain steadfast when practice gets difficult. So the vow of the bodhisattva can be a skillful strategy at first, helping us to move away from our self-centeredness. Practicing for the well-being of others, we take a step away from the local, small self, and move toward the realization of our boundless interconnectedness.

But ultimately, the radical optimist realizes that there is no self, no other—no one helping, no one being helped. The radical optimist becomes like a wooden puppet responding to the world, her limbs pulled by strings connected to the world's suffering. With time and experience we may develop a way of working with suffering rooted in raw and honest self-observation, and a view of reality that actualizes our awareness, equanimity, and compassion in seamless responsiveness to the world.

A person practicing in this way tries to exclude nothing from his heart. This often takes effort. It may take effort to mourn deeply, or to sit for hours doing nothing by the bedside of a dying child or a spouse dying of Alzheimer's. It may take effort to help others and not expect something in return. It may take effort to return our mind to practice. And it usually takes effort to bring energy and commitment to everything we do. Effort at its very core means letting go of fear. It is the courage and stamina to stay stripped to the bone and come face-to-face with what is. It is also manifesting wholeheartedness in the midst of the tight knot of suffering.

Effort gives our practice depth, character, strength, and resiliency. Can we hang in there when the situation is hopeless? Can we return again and again to our intention in doing this work? Can we be disciplined about self-care when the world around us seems to be crying out for attention? Can we be wholehearted in the midst of a heartless world?

Some years ago, walking across the Himalayas, I realized I would never make it over those mountains unless I let go of everything extra. That meant I had to lighten up my mind as well as my overloaded day pack. It all came down to one simple sentence: *Nothing extra!* Just as these two legs carried me across mountains, those same words carry me through complicated days. They always remind me to let go. They also remind me of the weightlessness and ease of a whole and dedicated heart.

Like souls in Dante's Purgatory, we carry the load of living and dying not simply to suffer but to learn to bear burdens lightly. The stones of hidden and silent wisdom become our teachers and companions along the way. They slow us down, ground us, and teach us about the weightiness and lightness of being. They ask us to stop and bend down low, touch the earth, and lift that which seems impossible to bear. Finally, making our backs strong, we open our eyes and discover that the stones are also beautiful.

When the Zen teacher Suzuki Roshi was dying, one of his students went to say goodbye. Standing at his bedside, the student asked his beloved teacher, "Where shall we meet?" The old dying man made a small bow from his bed, and then the gesture of a circle with his hand. I think he was telling his student they were meeting right then and there, in form and in emptiness as well. Past and future were in that moment, and at the same time the past and the future did not exist—and there was no place to meet that could be greater than the openness and intimacy of that very moment.

The radical optimist follows that intimate path, the path of impermanence through the great ocean of change. She is one with the tides of transition, unresisting. A true bodhisattva, she surfs on the waves of birth and death, with no destination in mind as she rides along, no other shore to head for. Having realized unconditional acceptance and cast aside her expectations, she coasts on the crest of the wildest waves with effortlessness and total involvement. Choice has disappeared in her world. She is thoroughly alive; and she gives no fear.

## MEDITATION

### Contemplating Our Priorities

The meditation that follows is a way we can explore our priorities, given that death may come at any time. Do this practice in a spirit of genuineness as you get in touch with your own impermanence in a very personal way. And don't hesitate to do it repeatedly; we may need to remind ourselves of our priorities in light of the fact that we don't know when our moment to die will come.

Please look at your life and your priorities: What is really important for you to do now? What do you want to complete or let go of right now? Offer your life to realizing these priorities.

Recall that we will all die. Each evening we go to bed and are convinced that we will wake up in the morning. We make plans for the next days, weeks, years, and even our old age. Most of us are probably convinced that we will live until old age. Most of us go to bed with this same feeling. Yet many people do not wake up in the morning. Death has taken them.

Now we have the opportunity to really set our priorities. Let the posture settle. Breathe deep into the body.

Imagine that you are an old person on your deathbed. Probably you have more wrinkles on your face, more stiffness in your limbs. Imagine your face as realistically as you can. Imagine that your breath is shallow; your body is tired and frail. Ask yourself, What goals would you like to have achieved by this stage of your life? What was most important for you in sustaining your daily life, your work, your relationships, your creativity, your spirit? What things are around you and where are you? Who is with you? What do you want your life to be like when you are an old person?

Now ask yourself, what can you do today so that you can be fulfilled at the end of your life? What do you need to let go of now to create a life filled with meaning? What do you need to take care of now so that old age may be a little easier and freer?

Imagine you are ten years older than you are now and are lying on your deathbed. How old are you? Who is standing by your bedside? What do you wish to have realized and achieved by this time? What are your inner and outer goals? What must you do today to achieve these goals? What must you let go of? What is wasting your time? What is important for you to do now? What hinders you from realizing what you really want for your life and the lives of those you love? What can you do today to support a good death?

Imagine that you are five years older than now and you are facing your death. Imagine you are peacefully in your bed and have just a few moments more to live. What do you want to have realized? What state of mind will support you in a peaceful death? What can you do now to help you strengthen your mind and heart so that you can bring this strength to your dying?

Now imagine that you will die in one year. You will probably not look very different from the way you do right now. You are lying peacefully in your bed and are prepared to die. What can you do at this moment to support your peaceful death? What gave your life meaning? What would you do differently right now, with the thought that you will lose your life in a year? What can you do tomorrow to realize the best death possible?

Imagine that you will die in one month. What would you change in your daily life? What do you need to do so you won't leave so many problems behind? What do you need to let go of, what habits do you need to break, in order to die peacefully? Which relationships need to be addressed? From whom do you need to ask forgiveness? Who do you need to forgive? What in yourself do you want to nurture at this time? What can you do tomorrow to support a peaceful death?

Now imagine that you will die next week. Who do you want around you, to share these last moments of your life? Who do you need to talk to about how you want to die and what should happen with your body? To whom do you want to express your deepest love and gratitude this week?

You go to bed tonight. No big deal. As you are falling asleep, you realize you are going to die. What is the most important thing you can do today in light of this possibility? What has been the biggest gift you have received in this life? With whom do you want to share your love for the last time?

Now take this love and thankfulness and go back to your breath. Gather this practice in the heart and mind and experience its essence. In your heart, share this practice with all beings, and hope that all beings will transform their fear of death and impermanence so that we can use our lives creatively to foster stability and beauty and to truly be of benefit to others.

# 5

## At Home in the Infinite
### *Dwelling in the Boundless Abodes*

AT THE TIME of the Buddha, there lived a monk named Tissa. Every morning he walked to the village and accepted whatever food people offered him. After doing his chores, he sat quietly in meditation, and in the evenings he recited prayers and studied.

One day Tissa fell sick. His whole body broke out in terrible pustules. The pustules gradually became bigger and bigger, and finally burst. But Tissa did not heal. Instead open sores covered his entire body, and the stench from the infection filled his tiny room.

At that time the Buddha happened to visit the monastery. He heard that Tissa had been abandoned by his fellow monks, who were repulsed by the sight and smell of his sick body. When the Buddha came to Tissa's hut, he opened the door and saw him lying in filth, his stinking robe sticking to the oozing sores.

The Buddha turned to his cousin and attendant, Ananda, and said, "Please boil some water over a fire and prepare an herbal bath."

When the water was ready, the Buddha gently washed the leaking sores on Tissa's body while Ananda washed and dried his soiled robes.

"Let us lay him on a clean bed," said the Buddha; so Ananda and the Buddha lifted Tissa and moved him. Then the Buddha held up his head and gave him fresh water to drink. Tissa opened his eyes and saw the

Buddha. "If you had not helped me, I would have died," the sick monk said. The Buddha then spent some time with Tissa, teaching him. Shortly after this careful tending, Tissa died, free in mind and body.

When the monks saw that the Buddha had cared so tenderly for Tissa, they bowed their heads in shame. Tears fell like rain from their eyes. "Tissa was our friend. We should have helped him," they said. "After all, we are monks."

The Buddha didn't judge them, but reminded them, "Monks, your father and mother are not here to take care of you. If you do not help one another, who will? Caring for one another is the same as taking care of me." Later the Buddha told his followers to help the sick with boundless loving-kindness, compassion, joy, and equanimity—what in Buddhism we call the four boundless abodes.

So many of us, at first, are like the fearful monks, feeling aversion and disgust in the presence of pain and suffering. We don't want to touch or care for our sick loved one—it's too strong a reminder of our own frailty and mortality, and of the anticipated loss of the loved one. But our awakening can begin to happen when we're finally drawn through the tight knot of suffering into the world of suffering around us. Eventually, compassion in action yields the golden fruit of real liberation.

Maintaining the story of "I" is exhausting. Defending the "I," promoting the "I," accumulating merit for the "I" can wear you out. On the other hand, selfless compassion can be energizing. We feel the world through itself, beyond the boundaries of our story line. We let our experience be, no longer trying to grasp what we like or to defend ourselves against what we fear. It takes a big heart to hold so much suffering. Sharon Salzberg, who developed many of the boundless-abode practices for us, says it takes a heart as wide as the world.

They're called "abodes" because each one is our home, the unconditional treasure always available to us, whether we're sick or dying or caring for those who grieve or face death. Generating them is the ultimate form of self-care. Practicing the four boundless abodes, discussed one at a time below, we realize that they are inherent to our basic nature. But by cultivating them deliberately in our activities, we can strengthen their presence within us. As that presence grows stronger, so does their boundless quality.

The first boundless abode, loving-kindness, allows us to transform our sense of separation and alienation into love. It is helpful to see that we are part of a greater whole, and a contemplative practice like loving-kindness can remind us that we're part of a continuum. We are more than our bodies, more than our thoughts, more than our feelings. Every time we identify with some fixed point in space or time, we close our hearts to the vastness of our being. Every time we narrow the vision of what we really are, we fall out of love and fall into fear.

As he lay dying, my father did not seem to be afraid. He had included old age, sickness, and death in his life even as he let go of it. He held the memory of my mother together with the presence of his new wife; his children, grandchildren, and great-grandchild together with nurses, doctors, and aides; and his discomfort alongside his sense of humor. Nothing was left out. As he gave away his life, his wisdom and kindness grew even deeper. He let go of opinions, concepts, and ideas. He let go of all of us. His true nature shone through his dissolving body as boundless love, completely free of clinging, for everyone around him.

Loving-kindness is supremely relational: it works only if it is offered, given away, or shared. We cannot bank love; it grows as we give it away. The more we give it away, the greater our capacity for love. This is how loving-kindness becomes limitless.

Years ago I participated in a small meeting with His Holiness the Dalai Lama. Several weeks beforehand, I had undergone eye surgery and my eyes had been subjected to radiation therapy. Unfortunately the radiologist did not fractionate the dose of radiation enough, and my eyes were badly burned. I was forced to wear bandages for several months while my raw eyes healed.

Since I was virtually blind, I considered not attending the meeting, but decided that I felt well enough to participate in some minimal way. His Holiness was very kind to me during the meeting, and after it was over, he asked if we could spend some time together. I knew that he was busy, so busy that he had given no private audiences to anyone during his six weeks in the United States, and I almost refused his invitation because I didn't want to bother him. In truth, I didn't feel worthy of his attention. But his assistant called and insisted that I come.

When I arrived in the private home where His Holiness was staying, he threw his arms around me in a big embrace. He then led me to a chair and asked me what had happened. After I briefly told him the story, he said that he hoped I had not suffered too much and that he was happy that my mind was clear and strong even though my eyes had been injured. He was kind without pity, loving without neediness. He then put his hands over the bandages and prayed.

At the moment when His Holiness touched the bandages, my fear disappeared, and I was truly happy. I had been touched by the essence of loving-kindness and compassion. It reminded me of something he had said in a talk: "My religion is kindness."

The second boundless abode is compassion. To develop compassion is to be open to suffering. This is a gradual process; through mindfulness we slowly begin to see the suffering in ourselves, and to become aware that everyone suffers in one way or another.

Compassion coupled with strength sustains our work with sickness, loss, and all the forms of suffering encountered in the experience of dying. Compassion is not an idealized state. It is the profound realization that we are not separate from one another, and it requires the ability to feel another's suffering. Like loving-kindness, it is fundamentally interactive and ultimately has no subject and no object. Loving-kindness and compassion are the perfume of interconnectedness, the fragrance of nonduality.

I have encountered great compassion in dying people. As Issan Dorsey lay dying, he felt the suffering of others deeply. He had always been a very open and experimental person, but his dying opened him to an even greater degree, allowing him to practice compassion with flawless humility.

The third boundless abode is sympathetic or noble joy. Sympathetic joy has three aspects: joy in the good fortune of others; joy in the virtue of others; and altruistic joy, that is, engendering joy to benefit others.

The first is that joy we feel when we realize that someone is in a favorable situation, that she is free from pain, that he has moved past his story and is finally relaxed and at ease. It is this kind of joy a caregiver feels when she hears that a beloved family member from far away can visit her dying patient, or when his illness has spontaneously receded from the shore of his life. This is the joy that fills the heart when good things happen to another.

Then there is the joy that one experiences by being in the presence of another's loving virtue. I felt and shared this when one day I visited a friend's child who was dying of cancer. I walked into her room and a smile broke out on this remarkable child's face that caught me in its light. I could not help but shine it back to her. She was pure joy, and at that moment, so was I. Maybe this is co-sympathetic joy, as her beauty and courage truly moved me and activated my intrinsic joy. This is the joy one feels when in the presence of a great teacher, a caring parent, a beloved friend, or a wonderful person. Their good heart activates your good heart.

The third form of sympathetic joy is the generation of joy to benefit others. One day, I walked into a hospital room of a man who had barely survived hypothermia and frostbite. Although he was doing adequately after his ordeal, he was depressed and irritable. Instead of identifying with his misery or consoling him, I found myself seeing through his suffering to a place that was free from it. I met his unhappiness with affectionate joy, and within minutes saw that he seemed to have been "infected" by my state of mind. He began to open up and smile at his unhappiness; then he began to relax and appreciate the care he was receiving. Altruistic joy can absorb and transform the energy of depression, self-pity, envy, competitiveness, resentment, and anger. It is an expression of compassion in action that is naturally free of narcissism and thoughts of oneself.

Sometimes fostering joy may be difficult when something good happens to another person, or when we meet a person of great integrity, or even when we realize that it may really help to generate joy to benefit another. We just don't seem to have the energy or will to arouse joy. Judgment and envy, comparisons and insecurity: these narrow our world and make sympathetic and altruistic joy difficult to experience. When a caregiver is worn to the bone, she might feel she doesn't have the resources to offer anything but negativity or dullness.

We can learn and practice offering joy to others, even though there might be a touch of pretending there in the beginning. Years ago, Sharon Salzberg assured me that it was OK to do these practices even if we are angry or depressed. From recent research in neuroscience we have learned that these areas of the brain can be intentionally cultivated. Like a violinist whose talent for playing increases with practice, we can also increase our joy with practice.

To someone who doubts that they can offer joy to a dying person, I say, "Why not?! Try anyway. See what happens in your own heart when you guide your behavior in accord with your intention." In the end, it's a lot less fatiguing to offer joy to others than sorrow.

So we can practice sympathetic joy. In sitting with a dying person, take the time to enjoy the simplest gifts of life, and see if a measure of joy can be engendered and shared in the present moment: the light of a late-autumn afternoon that floods the bedroom, the sound and smell of rain in the heat of summer, the notes of a piano concerto floating in from a close neighbor's house. Also look deeply into the person's life and recognize all the good that is there and mark it; this is taking joy in their virtue. Too often we just see pain, suffering, neurosis, a veritable textbook of misery before us. Look more deeply and find this one's good heart and let yourself meet it with your own.

The fourth boundless abode is equanimity. Some teachings even say that the other three boundless qualities all stem from equanimity. Equanimity's stability of mind allows us to be present with an open heart no matter how wonderful or difficult conditions are.

One moment your brother is alive; the next moment he's dead from a car accident. One morning you feel a lump in your breast, and your life changes in a way that you can't have imagined. One afternoon the doctor says you have inoperable cancer with three months to live. In a year, free of cancer, you have to put your life back together again. One day, your husband cannot find his way home. The mind is unraveling silently into dementia, and you and he find yourselves in unfamiliar and uncharted territory.

A student of Zen teacher Jay DuPont Roshi wrote a long e-mail to a wide circle of friends after the Zen master died, telling the story of his teacher's encounter with cancer. DuPont Roshi was diagnosed with melanoma on his left arm. When the doctor told him it was malignant, his response was to laugh. He said later that he'd always wondered how he would die; when he finally found out how it would happen, he said it was a relief!

DuPont Roshi then decided to let nature take its course and simply observe what was happening. The cancer grew, his arm swelled, and the roshi, who was left-handed, was in a great deal of pain. The doctor told him that soon, when the tumor got to a certain size, the pain might become unbearable.

Just as the tumor's progress seemed inevitable, it suddenly disappeared completely. The original mole remained, as well as some brown discoloration, which, he said, is the mark of anyone who has had melanoma. When asked why he thought the tumor went away, the roshi replied, "It is my experience that nothing can bear that kind of scrutiny."

What kind of mind and heart can stay so strong and open in the midst of all this chaos? Can we grieve fully without clinging to our grief, feel the postoperative pain without clinging to pain? Can we experience relief and joy without becoming attached to them, either? Can we be with the unknowable and open to trust at the same time?

A few years ago, I attended an elder student, who had suffered a massive heart attack and was taken to the emergency room near our Zen center. Hooked up to IVs, in the hush of a private space in the ER, she began to realize that she might be near death. As technicians stirred around her, she settled down into a quiet, open, and fearless state. She had been a child in Berlin during World War II and had vowed then to face death openly and with dignity. Those of us who sat with her in the ER could see her vows being actualized as the truth of her situation sank in.

As the days passed before her heart surgery, she kept this sense of boundlessness present as though it were a practice or a vow. All who spent time with her, from ambulance driver to surgeon, remarked on her equanimity and presence. She had faced death as a child; now as an older woman, her personal vow to face the truth with dignity and strength was thoroughly realized in the course of her crisis and recovery from surgery.

A few years later, my beloved student was diagnosed with a fast-growing cancer. She died six days after receiving the final diagnosis, and again her quiet presence and acceptance astounded those who cared for her. When she was told that nothing more could be done to help her, she simply dipped below the horizon and let go into the deep trough of peace. She went quickly, gracefully, her equanimity standing her in good stead.

Planting seeds of kindness, love, compassion, and joy helps us ride the waves of change without drowning. Equanimity, grounded in letting go, is the capacity to be in touch with suffering and at the same time not be swept away by it. Equanimity can be thought of as the state of being non-partial—not *impartial,* but *non*-partial. We hold all beings with the same heart, equally accepting of suffering and joy. Some people feel that equanimity must exclude caring. This is not the case. Rather, we love all beings equally, serene and steady as we ride the waves of change.

The truth of my experience is that the tender balance of equanimity can be easily lost. A profound quality of mind nurtured from the compost of our many failures, equanimity gives us the strong back that supports our tender heart. It is a jewel that shines with radiant compassion, giving us peaceful coolness.

This coolness and peace arise from a stable mind, a mind not caught in the fires of arousal, hatred, grasping, or confusion. With equanimity as our North Star, an alchemy of gratitude and well-being opens in our lives, rooted in our mindfulness practice. Our concentration and attention are steadier and sharper, and our ability to see the nature of truth, life, and death is deepened.

This traditional equanimity meditation helps us remember the truth of the nature of impermanence and cause and effect: "All beings are owners of their karma. Their happiness and unhappiness depend on their actions, not on my wishes for them." This might sound a little hard, a little ruthless, but it is true. One expression of equanimity is ruthless compassion. Another way to actualize equanimity is to cultivate the capacity to love all beings equally. A third dimension is to cultivate the capacity to uphold ourselves in the midst of the "full catastrophe."

Living in the home of boundlessness—giving nourishment to the skills of loving-kindness, compassion, altruistic joy, and equanimity—helps us experience being with dying as a practical way to turn suffering into freedom.

The philosopher Spinoza reminds us that all noble things are as difficult as they are rare. As we sit with dying people, as we ourselves die, please do not forget the vision of freedom from fear and suffering. The way to the realization of this vision is a noble journey that gives us strength and character precisely because it has so many obstacles. Let us use them all.

## Meditation

### Boundless Abodes for Living and Dying

Bringing together the strength of equanimity and the tenderness of compassion, the courage of presence and the openness of surrender, the following practices were crafted by teacher Sharon Salzberg, myself, and those participating in Upaya Zen Center's professional training program for compassionate end-of-life care.

The great gift of these Buddhist *brahmaviharas,* or "boundless abodes," is that they can live in the background of our mind and heart. When we lose balance, we can recall one of the phrases as a way to help us right ourselves, to be present for others, and to face suffering, our own and the suffering of others. And we can offer these phrases to those in our lives who are besieged by suffering—these practices are valuable for the dying as well as for caregivers. Choose the phrases that are personally meaningful to you; you can alter them in any way you wish or create your own.

To begin the practice, find as comfortable a position as possible, sitting or lying down. Take a few deep, soft breaths to let your body settle. Bring your attention to your breath and silently say your chosen phrase in rhythm with the breath. You can also experiment with allowing your attention to settle in the phrase without using the anchor of the breath. Feel the meaning of what you are saying, without trying or forcing anything. Let the practice carry you along.

Phrases that support loving-kindness:
- May loving-kindness flow boundlessly.
- May loving-kindness fill and heal your body.
- May the power of loving-kindness sustain you.

Phrases that nourish compassion:
- May you and all beings be free from pain and sorrow.
- May you take care of yourself.
- May all beings be free from the causes of suffering.

Phrases that engender sympathetic joy:
- May all beings be happy.
- May joy fill and sustain you.
- May your well-being continue.

Phrases that foster equanimity:
- Everyone must face her own situation.
- Your happiness or unhappiness depends upon your actions, not my wishes for you.
- May you accept things as they are.

# 6

## You Are Already Dying

*Realizing Impermanence, Selflessness, and Freedom*

H OW MANY PEOPLE who will die today even know that this will
be the last day of their lives? I think of friends who have died
without completing projects, without having had the opportunity to say words of goodbye to a spouse or a child, without having forgiven a friend. Again, we still don't believe it can happen to us.

We may take care of a dying friend and make the natural mistake of
thinking ourselves separate from her experience. In our minds, we may
divide ourselves from her: "She is dying; I'm the caregiver." But in reality,
we're joined by the bonds of impermanence. Maybe it's too disturbing to
say to yourself, I am dying, too. But as noted in chapter 4, the truth is you
are already dying. So am I. We're all linked by the inevitability of loss and
death, even if we seem to be easily meandering down the road of living.

Every one of us has had to give up something we loved. We've sacrificed
cherished plans or dreams, felt grief and loss. Already, all of us have experienced impermanence, which is just another form of dying. What hasn't
changed in one way or another? Everything is always changing. Even the
sun, a symbol of immortality, is a star that will someday be extinguished.

If we start training ourselves to observe the changing nature of our
everyday situations, we can be on our way to freedom from suffering.

Accepting impermanence and our shared mortality requires loosening the story knot: letting go of our concepts, ideas, and expectations around how we think dying ought to be. It also calls us to "practice dying"—that is, to let go, surrender, and give away, in the best of worlds, to practice generosity. We can do this now; at any time, we can start practicing dying. And if we do, we might also start to perceive the interdependence of suffering and joy—that life and death are not separate but intertwined like roots deep in the earth.

During a meditation retreat, one man who suffered from AIDS-related lymphoma experienced a profound insight into the nature of impermanence. Several months later, as active dying unfolded, he was hospitalized. The tumors pressed against nerves and caused excruciating pain. When I visited him, he expressed gratitude for having seen that all things do change, because he knew this would include the experience of his pain. In a quiet voice, he told me that if he thought the pain were permanent, he would go crazy. He clearly and bravely stated that he knew that, at the least, death would release him from the stabbing pain that could not be managed by drugs. Realizing impermanence, including the truth of his mortality, gave him strength to accept pain and let go of the feelings of desperation that had begun to overcome him.

When I am sitting with a dying person, I sometimes hear the following words inside me: "Whatever suffering this person is experiencing, it will change." Maybe for better, maybe for worse. Change is inevitable—that's impermanence. And at the same time, it is necessary to be fully there for the often overwhelming and raw truth of moment-to-moment suffering.

The awareness of impermanence can serve to deepen our commitment to living a life of value and meaning. Many traditions teach the inevitability of death as the bedrock for the entire spiritual path. Plato told his students, "Practice dying." The Christian monks of medieval Europe ritually whispered to one another, *"Memento mori"* ("Remember death"). And one Buddhist sutra tells us, "Of all footprints, that of the elephant is supreme. Of all meditations, that on death is supreme."

Death, however, is not usually regarded in contemporary Western culture as a teacher with whom to spend time, but rather as a looming biological and even moral failure to be denied and avoided. We do not hold a collective view of death as redemptive or liberating, but see it as an enemy to be beaten or, at best, a bad situation to be endured. The possibility of realization at the moment of death is not part of the story our culture is telling us; so death has little or nothing to offer most of us, and under those circumstances, it is often justifiably feared. When we distance ourselves from death in this unnatural way, it would seem that the only solution to the problem of dying is to avoid it at all costs! And costly it often is—as many of our health-care dollars are spent in the last six months of our lives.

To practice dying in our culture is not often seen as safe or advisable. But if our culture were to recognize that death and life are inseparable, our approach to both might be quite different. For one thing, we wouldn't be in denial, suffering collective grief and anxiety over the constant losses and changes we experience in life. Perhaps, from the great spiritual traditions of the past, we can retrieve a vision of dying that makes it possible for us to embrace the unknown without being paralyzed with fear, and to embrace the truth of impermanence as we open our arms to the world. As one old friend said to me, "Change is inevitable, growth is optional."

Up until we have received a catastrophic diagnosis or lost someone we love, we might take life for granted. When we receive a diagnosis that we have just a little while to live, or when our closest friend dies, our focus may sharpen, at least for a while, and we begin to examine our lives and our fate. We may choose to make our remaining days into a medical project, or bring our attention to psychological and spiritual issues in the search for meaning, taking care of our relationships and being of benefit to others.

The interesting thing is that some of us will not begin inner work until we are in the heart of suffering. And this may be a little bit too late, for the habits of mind that drive us are deeply rooted, and to uproot them in a matter of days, weeks, or months might not be so easy, although it is possible. Or, as Zen teacher Richard Baker Roshi told me, "Enlightenment is an accident; practice makes you accident-prone."

We can be prone to awakening or inclined toward suffering. This might sound so obvious, but I have always wondered why so many of us do not bother to take care of the mind and heart until the "last minute"? Why do we move away from opportunities that will mature us? Why not take this precious opportunity now, instead of waiting for a catastrophic diagnosis? What does it take for us to wake up? Sooner or later, as Robert Louis Stevenson once noted, everyone sits down to a banquet of consequences.

One important practice to help settle us into an awareness of impermanence is that of generosity. Since we'll lose all our possessions and connections when we die, why not begin giving away what we have right now? Instead of holding on tightly to all that we think "belongs" to us, we can practice being generous and giving away the things we love to others. One close friend gave away much of his fortune and land before he died. He died peacefully at the venerable age of ninety-two, after a morning at the office, again giving away money to others. As he grew older, he felt that every day was an opportunity to lighten his burden, including the burden of his wealth. He liberated huge amounts of money in the course of his lifetime; as he did so, he also seemed to liberate himself. This wonderful elder felt that generosity would establish a pattern in his heart and mind to help him let go of life when the time was ready.

The realization of the imminence of death can be a direct path to the discovery of meaning in life. For many individuals the worst suffering is meaninglessness. Strangely enough, suffering and dying can often restore meaning and depth to lives that have been bereft. As Holocaust survivor Viktor Frankl wrote, death is what gives life meaning. "I always want to be terminal," one cancer patient told me, close to death. His diagnosis returned to him pieces of his life lost when he was healthy. In dying, he reclaimed unlived parts of his life that were to benefit not only him but everyone around him as well. He reminded me that we are all terminal.

But death's door can look very narrow, too, and we can become panicked when it opens toward us, particularly when there is nowhere to go except through it. If we believe that we are nothing but this body, we can be cast into the valley of fear when the body begins to unbind. If we think we are alone in dying, or we feel lost in grief, our feelings of isolation can cloud and shrink our view. If we perceive the pain we suffer as solid, unchangeable, and eternal, our experience can turn hard and claustrophobic.

There are three important gates that can open our view to a bigger horizon, if we find our way to them. Opening the first gate reveals that everything is impermanent, even—especially—living in this human body. The second gate, when it opens, shows us that there is no separate self. And behind the third gate gleams the luminous nature of our own mind.

My friend Rob Lehman, diagnosed with non-Hodgkin lymphoma, said that the prospect of death shed light on the shape and tenacity of his ego. In the waves of fear and denial that washed over him, he recognized that the very "self" he was trying to make solid with his story was actually the author of his suffering. Now he could see himself and others as one and the same, coming together and falling apart according to the circumstances of any given moment.

Rob began to practice with the psalmist prayer—"Help me to know the shortness of life, that I may gain wisdom of heart"—and realized he had always been seeking something greater than what he already had, and had suffered accordingly. With death as his new companion, his grasping and attachment withered. He began to let go into what he called "a greater Self, which in turn dissolves into an even greater love for the world." What he had before sought outside himself he now discovered within.

He shared with friends that his insights had resulted in a profound shift of identity, writing, "My identity is not merely the sum total of the many dimensions of my personality. At its most transparent, it is the integration of all I am with all everyone and everything is, and this integrated whole is held by a mystery of Generous Love. As I allow myself to feel the impact of this shift, I realize that I do not die when I die."

To realize that we suffer because we see ourselves as permanent and separate is so important. Compassion flowers from the realization that we are not separate and have no fixed identity. When we let ourselves love, we no longer resist the suffering of others. Lama Lodro Dorje reminds us that love is a meltdown. That meltdown establishes a more unified space of brilliance, goodness, and sadness. We can no longer protect ourselves from others' suffering. We experience it simply as suffering—not "mine" or "yours"—just as, if we hurt our left hand, our right hand takes care of it. The right hand and left hand just do what naturally needs to be done, and the space between those hands holds the human heart.

When my father lay dying, I did not expect anything from him. The right hand was taking care of the left. And at the same time, my heart was broken open. After his death, I sat with his body, wondering where his so-called self had gone. Is there any part of him that is fixed and permanent? Then I clearly saw my father's selfness as non-local. Today, he lives in his children and grandchildren. His good life inspired many people, and his aspirations live on in them. He is in the earth of the Zen center where I live, where gardens have been planted and tended. He is in the words I write, the talks I give; in the good works of my sister and half brother and their children and grandchildren. He is now everywhere. He had, in fact, always been everywhere—but I had seen him as local, not universal, until he died.

Two days before he died, my father was approached by a nurse, who asked him, "How are you feeling, Mr. Halifax?" And without hesitation he replied, "Everything."

In our culture, with its strong emphasis on personal identity and biography, many of us find it hard to understand what "no-self" means. But we as beings are not separate from one another. We are interconnected, interdependent, and interpenetrating. At our Zen center, we chant this food offering together before we eat:

> Earth, water, fire, air, and space
> combine to make this food.
> Numberless beings gave their lives and labor
> that we may eat.
> May we be nourished that we may nourish life.*

In that simple meal blessing, I can see earth, water, fire, air, and space. There I see plants, soil, pollinating bees, insects, human labor, and an infi-

---

* Composed by Joan Halifax.

nite chain of relationships. We, too, are made up of earth, water, fire, air, and space. All of us are interconnected with the sun, moon, wind, and rain, and will someday return to the mother elements. And all of us are also connected in the stream of basic goodness.

If we are able to realize that we aren't separate from others, that we have no inherent identity, and that nothing is fixed in time and space, our suffering diminishes or even ceases. Yet seeing is believing. We need a direct and personal experience of interconnectedness and impermanence for them to be made true and real in our own lives.

Although one friend of mine was dying of ovarian cancer, she was still obsessed with her work as a graphic designer. Hooked up on an IV as well as to her computer, she was finding it very difficult to face the end of her life. One day, at the request of her daughter, a Tibetan doctor came to visit her. He instructed my friend to sit on a mountaintop and look into the sky as an antidote to her habitual fixation on her work and her fear of dying. Later in the week when she had regained a little strength, she asked to be taken to the ski basin high above Santa Fe. She and her daughter sat for an hour in near silence, as they watched the clouds moving across the late-afternoon Southwestern sky. At her mother's memorial service, her daughter told us that this was the pivotal moment in their relationship. The intimacy that had opened up for them was born in that quiet afternoon in the Sangre de Cristo Mountains, and she felt it was that intimacy and spaciousness that had helped her mother die.

Whether we open to the sky or sea or simply sit in stillness and silence, when we move away from the familiar ground of ideas, mental chatter, and compulsive work that has seemed to support us, we can discover the space that is our true home, our original dwelling place.

Bring yourself to this place where you already are, your original dwelling place. A bigger view is available to you right now, in the unfiltered experience of this very moment—an experience below the rippling of concepts and deeper than language. Just sit down and breathe. Take a moment to stabilize your mind, allowing your natural wisdom to arise. I promise that you will see for yourself that nothing, including your own individual identity, exists in the absolute sense in terms of an unchanging, permanent truth. With our view of reality wide and clear, we discover that inexpressibly vast horizon of not-knowing, shining in the dawn of silence and surrender.

# MEDITATION

## *The Nine Contemplations*

Legend has it that Confucius was given the task of stringing a nine-faceted jewel—this meant that he would have to pass the soft thread through nine impossibly tight turns at the jewel's center. The penalty for failure to accomplish this task was death. Our philosopher could not figure out how to do this terribly difficult thing. Time was short, but no solution presented itself. He found himself in the land of the inconceivable.

Then, surprisingly, he encountered a mysterious young girl in a mulberry bush. She told him that he must discover a secret. Now the word for "secret" in Chinese sounds a lot like the word for "honey." In a twinkle, Confucius, without thinking, had the solution. He fastened a thread to the body of an ant. He then lured the ant with honey to enter the twisted bore of the jewel. In this way, the ant negotiated the nine hard turns of the narrow path, the jewel was threaded, and the life of Confucius was given back to him.

The Zen teacher Jan Chozen Bays reminds us that this jewel is our very life, our very mind, but like the ant we are blind to it, and like Confucius, it presents a big problem for us. The narrow, twisting path is the way of initiation, the place of passage that brings life to our life if we are able to find our way through it. But we have to discover the way ourselves. The thread is also our life. One purpose of life is to let this fine and flexible part of our nature be pulled through the narrows to liberate our real wisdom, tugged blindly not by knowledge but by innocent sweetness.

The nine contemplations that follow offer a way to explore our vulnerability and the inevitability of death. They are perspectives on living and dying that were explored by the great eleventh-century monk and scholar Atisha Dipankara Shrijnana. The practice Atisha developed asks us to question what we are doing in our life at this very moment and to see what is important, in the light of our mortality. The simple truths outlined in this practice are meant to arouse awareness in relation to how we are living our life. What are we doing now to deepen our experience? How are we now working with our own fear and suffering and that of others? What are we doing to prepare not only for liberation at the moment of death but for liberation at this very moment?

The nine contemplations are like a weather report warning us of a storm in our future. The warning cannot predict exactly when or how the storm will hit, but it does tell us that the storm is inevitable and that we'd best prepare for it. That being the case, why not prepare for it now? Why not cultivate a way of life that trains us in being awake—in living and in dying? Accepting the truth of the inevitability of death is how we can begin to go beyond fear and fully engage with our lives.

Find a comfortable position to sit in. Allow your body to relax and calm down. If you want to, close your eyes. Let your mind settle. Bring your attention to your breath. Please consider each contemplation deeply.

## THE FIRST CONTEMPLATION

All of us will die sooner or later.

*Death is inevitable; no one is exempt.*

*Holding this thought in mind, I abide in the breath.*

Even though it may be difficult for you to realize that someday you will die, there is no way around it. Not a single being—no matter how spiritually evolved, powerful, wealthy, or motivated—has escaped death. The Buddha, Jesus, and Muhammad did not evade it, nor will you or I. All the gifts of your life—education, wealth, status, strength, fame, gender, friends, and family—will make no difference. Death lends profound equality to us all.

When the mind wanders away from contemplating the inevitability of death, call it back. You might resist by drifting in thought or turning to fantasy. Watch what your mind does to escape this simple fact. Can you face the truth that Death pervades every cell in your body? Bring your attention back to this opportunity to touch the truth, realizing that you will die, that each being precious to you will die, that each person and each creature now on earth will die.

## THE SECOND CONTEMPLATION

My life span is ever-decreasing.

*The human life span is ever-decreasing; each breath brings us closer to death.*

*Holding this thought in mind, I delve deeply into this truth.*

Your life span lessens every moment. Life flows, for better or worse, between birth and death, these two points of change. Your continual movement toward death never stops. Every breath you take in and give out, every word you speak, every thought you think, brings you closer to this destination. Every step you take brings you closer to your final resting place.

As you consider this, notice what comes up in your mind. If the mind attempts to divert you, call yourself back to the truth that your life is limited. Appreciate what you have now, and admit that there may be no tomorrow. What are you doing with this life now to live it fully and to support a sane and gentle death? What are you doing to help others? What gives your life meaning?

## THE THIRD CONTEMPLATION

Death comes whether or not I am prepared.

*Death will indeed come, whether or not we are prepared.*

*Holding this thought in mind, I enter fully into the body of life.*

Most of us will meet death without having strengthened our awareness of our true nature. How much time do you now spend training and stabilizing your mind? How many of your thoughts are you aware of? How many are about freedom from suffering and death? How often do you remember that death will come? We spend so much time eating, drinking, grooming, playing, working, sleeping. We conduct business, make and spend money, and tend our relationships. Most of us are doing so little to prepare ourselves for death. What kind of practice will strengthen your mind? What can you do to wake up in this life? Is your capacity to give attention to the mind and body adequate to meet the challenge of dying? You can ready yourself right now. Before the journey, please make the best arrangements possible for this destination called death.

### THE FOURTH CONTEMPLATION

My life span is not fixed.

*Human life expectancy is uncertain; death can come at any time.*

*Holding this thought in mind, I am attentive to each moment.*

Think of the many beings who died this day. How many of them really thought they were going to die today? Do you really think that you know how much time you have left? Death can come at any moment. You could die this afternoon; you could die tomorrow morning; you could die on your way to work; you could die in your sleep. Most of us try to avoid the sense that death can come at any time, but its timing is unknown to us. Can we live each day as if it were our last? Can we relate to one another as if there were no tomorrow?

### THE FIFTH CONTEMPLATION

Death has many causes.

*There are many causes of death—even habits and desires are precipitants.*

*Holding this thought in mind, I consider the endless possibilities.*

The causes of death are infinite. You can die because of a storm or an accident; you can die of cancer, heart disease, diabetes, old age. You can die of fear or of a broken heart. Even if you have been diagnosed with a so-called terminal illness, it may not be the cause of your death. Many conditions bring death, and the forces that sustain life are few. Watch what your mind does when you contemplate the truth that death can come through so many doors. Do you try to avoid this thought, or are you able to consider the possibilities?

## THE SIXTH CONTEMPLATION

My body is fragile and vulnerable.

*The human body is fragile and vulnerable; my life hangs by a breath.*

*Holding this thought in mind, I attend as I inhale and exhale.*

You may feel as if you will live forever—or growing older, seeing other people die, you may know differently. Life literally hangs by a breath. Breathe in. After exhaling, consider the possibility that you might not be able to inhale again. When breath no longer enters your body, then your life span has ended, and you will die. Say to yourself, "This life is fragile and completely dependent on my breath." Can you allow yourself to really know this? The beating of your heart and the activity of your brain give life to your life. An accident, a moment of violence, a single misstep can bring your life to a surprising and rapid end. Does knowing how vulnerable and fragile you are turn your mind toward living?

## THE SEVENTH CONTEMPLATION

My material resources will be of no use to me.

*At the time of death, material resources are of no use.*

*Holding this thought in mind, I invest wholeheartedly in practice.*

Imagine lying on your deathbed, growing weaker by the moment. You have spent your life earning money, accumulating possessions. You have a beautiful home, bank accounts, an expensive car, fine clothes and jewelry. But on the threshold of death, what good are they? Every single penny, every single item must be left behind—all the comforts for which you worked so hard. They will be utterly useless at the hour of your death—or worse than useless, impediments to surrendering fully. Can you see yourself clinging to your story and identity? Consider that all of your cherished objects will be redistributed when you die. Everything you have accumulated will be given away to friends and relatives. Some of it may end up in a thrift store or a junk pile. Now ask, What is a sound investment to make in this life? What will be important at the moment of death? Release attachment and practice generosity now.

### THE EIGHTH CONTEMPLATION

My loved ones cannot save me.

*Our loved ones cannot keep us from death; there is no delaying its advent.*

*Holding this thought in mind, I exercise non-grasping.*

It is only natural to turn to friends and family at times of difficulty. However, the people whom you love cannot keep death from you, and strong attachments may produce sorrow and clinging, which will only make dying more difficult. Your loved ones are powerless in the face of your death. No matter how kind and adept your friends might be, ultimately there is nothing they can do for you when you are dying. What really is going to help at the moment of your death?

### THE NINTH CONTEMPLATION

My own body cannot help me when death comes.

*The body cannot help us at death; it, too, will be lost at that moment.*

*Holding this thought in mind, I learn to let go.*

You have spent so much time working on your body—feeding it, watering it, exercising it, dressing and undressing it, enjoying and not enjoying it. You may spend hours thinking about your body, looking at it in a mirror, evaluating its appearance, trying to make it look younger and more beautiful. This body has been your constant companion, sometimes a friend, sometimes an enemy. You have experienced so much pain in it and so much pleasure. You treasure it. You despise it. And at the moment of death, you lose it. Can you feel your dependence on your body, your attachment to it? Can you see how holding on to your body might torment you? Can you understand why there is so much fear, so much clinging to life, such anger in anticipation of giving up life? Can you feel compassion for yourself and for others? What is really important in light of this truth that we cannot hold on to this body? What can you do to prepare yourself to face your death skillfully, and to help others face theirs?

# PART TWO

## Giving No Fear

AT Upaya Zen Center, we have a beautiful bronze statue of Mahapajapati, the Buddha's foster mother. Her expression is serene, and she holds her right hand upraised, palm turned outward, in the gesture known as "giving no fear." As we step over the threshold into being with dying, the most important gift we can give others and ourselves is the gift of no fear.

Recognizing our interconnectedness is the heart of giving no fear. We are linked together in our blood, in the stringing of our nerves through us and between us. Life connects us to one another, as do suffering, joy, death, and enlightenment. When we see our fear clearly and step through it by reconnecting with the moment and our sameness, fear may evaporate and, in its place, compassion can bloom. When I am sitting with a dying person, I cannot in deepest reality separate myself from him. Our unconditional goodness connects us.

Often, though, the transition out of life can be unpredictable and chaotic. It is a time of great uncertainty for a dying person. It may be that nothing we have relied on is there to support us. The best and often the only thing to do is to let go and, as Bernie Glassman Roshi teaches, bear witness to the change—to be with what is without resistance and allow for the inevitable changes around dying to happen freely. We can entrust ourselves to reality and learn to show up, simply being present for whatever is offered, whether the underbelly of suffering, the mystery of transcendence, or the truth of the ordinary.

On this path of bearing witness to dying, can we give no fear? Can we give up our tight control strategies, our ideas of what it means to "die well"—concepts that can blind us to the experience of those we are trying to help—and really let the dying person take the lead? And, equally importantly, can we care for ourselves as we wish to care for others? Whether you are dying or giving care, each of these depends on your fully letting go into the present moment, the mother of awareness, bearing deep witness.

In dying, our body and mind unbind along with our relationship to others and things; and in that unraveling we have a chance to connect with something greater than the small self so identified with our sense of being separate. Time as we have known it flows into the big ocean of timelessness. In this altered, intensified state, the threshold experience pulls us down and in, and this serves as an initiation that can destroy our attachment to that little self. Dying to our story, we pass through loss, and possibly the relief of letting go.

Bearing witness calls us continually to cross the threshold of our story. Out of our expectations, beliefs, and fears, most of us fabricate a version of how things are. We defend ourselves against the fear of pain with our story; we like to use it as a buffer against impermanence, trying to protect ourselves from the fact that death comes for everyone, often without warning. To acknowledge our individual small story and then to go beyond it expresses true compassion—sharing the suffering and joy of others while being in touch with our own situation as well.

In the passage from life to death, what you will go through is not a story, or an idea that is somewhere "out there." Your old identity is thrashed like grain, and a new life may grow from the brokenness of your past and the breaking open of the present. Dying and being with dying are threshold experiences with the potential to destroy our self-clinging as they liberate us into a larger space.

# 7

## Fictions That Hinder and Heal
### *Facing Truth and Finding Meaning*

W HEN I WAS a young woman working on my doctorate, I spent time in the hospital with an old woman who had breast cancer. Just before she died, she told me that you can never really know what dying is about until it is happening to you. Her eyes said even more than her words. All the stories she'd once told herself about the way she would die shattered against the reality of what her dying was really like.

Although we can become familiar with the physiology, psychology, and spirituality of dying, we cannot know death until it is happening to us. However, we can reconnoiter the territory. We can investigate the many little deaths and births we experience in daily life, exploring loss, change, and impermanence. We can try to stabilize our minds through spiritual practice. And we can listen to the stories we tell ourselves about death and perhaps loosen the knot that binds the stories to us by reaching deep inside each story to its very heart.

Many of us understandably try to find a way around the truth that we will eventually die. T.S. Eliot points out that we humans "cannot bear very much reality."* Instead of preparing for death, we might try to control or

---

* T. S. Eliot, "Burnt Norton," in *Four Quartets* (London: Faber & Faber, 1941).

avoid it, telling ourselves stories about living to a ripe old age in hopes of feeling more solid, sure, and safe. These stories can either be harmful fabrications or what psychologist James Hillman called "healing fictions," stories that help us find meaning in living and dying.*

If we create the story that death is a tragedy and a defeat, for example, this might well color our experience of dying and our relationship with dying people. Or, instead, if we create a story of death as a great adventure, and it turns out that our mental and physical faculties are diminished and we are miserable as we approach death, we might wonder what happened to our so-called "good death."

We don't know how or when we will die—even as we are actually dying. Death, in all its aspects, is a mystery, and our stories might open the door to the unknown or help us fool ourselves and those around us.

One friend in her late eighties, a wild-haired optimist, sensed that she was on her way out. Her heart was struggling to keep up with her. But she had a humorous and somewhat romantic view of her dying and wanted to be surrounded by her younger friends as she died—in fact, she wanted a party. Breaking through the fatigue of congestive heart failure was indomitable will. If anybody could plan a deathbed scene, it was her. But as it turned out, she died one night in her sleep, free of her story. Her friends experienced a certain amount of disappointment when they discovered she had gone her merry way without them. They had the party anyway.

A young man with whom I worked felt he was ready to die and stopped taking his medications, with the idea that he would die a "noble" death a few days later. Even though we told him that the body dies in its own time and we could not predict what would happen, he found our counsel hard to accept, and he stuck to his story that he would die a quick and heroic death.

As the days passed and he did not die, this young man became more and more miserable. He had said valiant goodbyes to his family and friends; he was ready to die, and he did not want things to drag on.

Four months later his patience had been thoroughly tested, and he had

* James Hillman, *Healing Fiction* (New York: Spring Publications, 1994).

none left. His death was not going to happen the way he wanted it to, and he felt his "story" had betrayed him. No amount of presence, support, love, and common sense could allay his anger, as he shifted into another story, this one focusing on him as a victim. He had lost control of his death, along with everything else in his life.

Those of us who were his caregivers had done our best to be there as he fought with frustration and physical pain. He was a young man who had always planned carefully and carried out his plans with commitment. Now this same energy had become an obstacle to living his dying. He had attended so-called good deaths of friends and expected his death to be like theirs. He had a definite idea of how things should be, and they were not working out that way. Finally, on what proved to be the morning of his death, after a difficult last struggle against the ideas that opposed his reality, he finally gave it all up.

Caring for this young man, I asked myself if there really is such a thing as a "good death." I couldn't call his death good or bad. He did it his way, and in retrospect, though it was at times hard for him and hard for us, it was an amazing journey. I had to respect his strange valor.

Each person dies in her or his own way. The young man, whose story I told above, from one point of view seemed to die too late. But was it too late? Did the shift in his story from hero to victim lead him to yet a third perspective, one that was free of bad and good, hero and victim?

As his final hours unfolded, everything seemed to drop away from him, including his suffering, including his story. He slipped beneath the wave of life and dove out of sight. In the end, I could not evaluate his journey. I simply felt love for my young friend, and over the years my respect for him has increased.

The concept of a good death can put unbearable pressure on dying people and caregivers, and can take us away from death's mystery and the richness of not knowing. Our expectations of how someone should die can give rise to subtle or direct coerciveness. And no one wants to be judged for how well she dies!

"Death with dignity" is another concept that can become an obstacle to what is really happening. Dying can be very undignified. Often, it's not dignified at all, with soiled bedclothes and sheets, bodily fluids and flailing, nudity and strange sexuality, confusion and rough language—all common enough in the course of dying. The stories we tell ourselves— good death, death with dignity—can be unfortunate fabrications that we use to try to protect ourselves against the sometimes raw and sometimes wondrous truth of dying.

Our stories can also be bridges to freedom as well. There are many powerful stories around dying and of "enlightened deaths" that leave us with renewed inspiration and determination. So many remarkable experiences of the deaths of great teachers have forever inspired and influenced their students. The stories of graceful deaths of friends remind us that death can teach us about the strength of the human spirit and the possibility of death being truly a liberation. These stories can be important life-giving legacies.

Stories can give our suffering meaning, our dying depth, our grieving perspective. They can open a door or reveal a path. I have learned over and over again that it is liberating to make visible our stories long before active dying begins, and then to let go of these narratives as the presence of what is really happening unfolds.

So, please, become aware of the stories around death—the stories we are telling ourselves, the stories our culture tells us, the stories that our health-care institutions have created. Please direct awareness toward what you might tell yourself about dying and death. Become familiar with how you might shield yourself from the truth of death with certain ideas or how you can let the story be a raft taking you to the other shore.

Learn to access that still inner space where wisdom rests, the wisdom that allows us to question, see, and learn from everything within and around us. This wisdom embraces the story, can inform the story, and is not the story.

As one woman was dying, she expressed relief that everyone around her was so very calm. The wild search for a cure for her cancer had taken her to many extremes as she clung to her story that she would die of old age. She still felt the momentum of that search as she approached active dying. Then, one day, in an instant, she seemed to stop. Her busyness simply came to an end. Those of us sitting with her felt the shift as she joined us like an island sailing into a stable continent. She finally settled down to die, with a narrative of acceptance supporting her journey toward the unknown. This woman's new story gave her the strength to let go.

Our practice of not-knowing points to an openness in perspective, an openness that is deeper than a story, deeper than our expectations, deeper than our wishes, deeper than our personality, deeper than cultural constructs. Being with dying gives us a precious opportunity to question all our stories, to drop the old harmful fabrications that no longer serve us, and to transform our stories into healing fictions that help us show up for our living and dying.

# MEDITATION

## Bearing Witness to Two Truths

### PART ONE: SEEING PURELY

Seeing purely means that we lend nonjudgmental presence fully to who each person is. We want to see this person's deepest awakened nature, while also seeing and respecting their experience of suffering. This is the essence of the practice that follows: how to be fully with the truth of suffering and simultaneously with the truth of each person's basic goodness. We first open up the resource of our own good heart, and then lean into the basic goodness of another, looking through and past the acid-etched weariness, anger, or unhappiness to the place that has been and always will be free of the marks of misery.

You can practice with this at any time and in any place. For now, try it while sitting in a chair. Sit across from a friend or imagine your friend opposite you and gently close your eyes. Let your body be comfortable and adjust your posture as the need arises. Bring awareness to your breath as you continue to settle. Breathe deep into your belly. Let yourself relax as your mind stays with the in-breath and the out-breath. As thoughts, feelings, and sensations arise, let go of them, keeping it very simple, just being with the breath. As you breathe, feel yourself relaxing in such a way that you are deeper than your personality and your identity. There is nowhere to go, nothing to do. You are presence without any object or objective, presence deeper than personality.

Now imagine yourself as a three- or four-year-old child. See yourself at a time when you were happy and free. Perhaps you can recall a photo of yourself, or bring to mind the face of an innocent, joyful child. Feel what it must be like to be this child. Look out through her eyes, eyes that are clear and bright, fresh and immaculate. These innocent eyes are always here in you. You are these eyes of no judgment and no prejudice. Feel at peace with this simplicity.

Now, open your eyes and gaze into the chest area of your friend sitting across from you, or visualize your suffering friend in your mind. Keep it very simple. If you start to feel a need to do anything, close your eyes and return to that image of the child's innocent eyes.

Let your awareness be with your friend's breathing. You may synchronize your breathing with him or her if you wish. Simply be present. See out through nonjudgmental eyes at the one sitting across from you. Be aware of your breath and the rise and fall of your friend's chest. Just gaze out through gentle eyes.

When you feel ready, allow your gaze to move to your friend's throat area. Do not grasp or retreat. Simply look openly and quietly at your friend's throat. A little more of her or his identity is being revealed to you. Be with your breath. Keep your vision soft and accepting as you raise your eyes to gaze into the eyes of this friend sitting across from you. Notice if you feel uncomfortable with the contact. If you do, go inside and remember the child whose eyes you were looking through. When you feel stable, let your eyes gently open and look at your friend from a place that is deeper than your personality.

When you feel you have been present for this person at this moment, allow yourself to see your friend becoming young like a small child, full of anticipation and good intentions. See this person as she or he might have been when very young and free of suffering. Imagine that this fresh and hopeful being is still alive in your friend. Look without judgment or story. See this person's eyes as luminous and innocent, free of fear and sorrow. See your friend's good heart and immaculate nature from the place inside yourself that is deeper than your personality. Keep it very simple. See through innocent eyes. If you feel as though you are beginning to fixate, close your eyes and return to your breath.

Now, in your imagination, bring your friend into the present. Seeing this one as he or she is now, see that his or her original nature is still here. Look through open eyes to the truth of this person's life. Be aware of the joy and suffering; and be aware that there is a place inside that is free of all conditions.

Maintain this vision of purity of heart, relaxing and closing your eyes as you return your awareness to your breath.

## Part Two: Bearing Witness

If you do the following practice with a friend who is present, you and your partner will decide which one of you will first bear witness and who will speak. The one bearing witness is asked to listen to the speaker. The listener will say nothing, do nothing, but simply be present. Do not touch the speaker; do not offer comfort. Trust in your presence to be enough. (You can also imagine what your friend might say to you, and be as present as possible for his or her words.)

The speaker takes a few moments to recall an experience of suffering. He or she then speaks about this experience for five minutes without interruption. When he or she is done, the speaker in turn bears witness for the listener, who now speaks. Complete the practice by offering your gratitude to each other.

When you have decided who will speak first, close your eyes and relax. The listener brings his or her breath deep into the belly. The speaker contemplates an experience of suffering. As the speaker begins to talk, the listener breathes deeply and evenly, gently being present for the speaker. The listener should be aware if impulses arise to comment, give advice, or change or fix the situation. We don't act on these impulses when simply bearing witness.

At the end of five minutes, the listener might ring a small bell, or nod to the speaker. If you are the speaker, please finish what you are saying at this time. After the five-minute bell is rung, there is a brief pause, and then the speaker can share with the listener how it felt to be listened to in this way. After a few minutes of reply, the listener shares with the speaker how it felt to listen in this way. Then participants reverse roles.

This practice, even when done in imagination only, can be powerful training for being present as a caregiver without trying to console, relieve, or save the suffering one, but simply bearing witness to whatever arises.

# 8

## The Two Arrows

### *I Am in Pain and I Am Not Suffering*

WHEN I TEACH caregivers, I often ask participants which concerns them the most about dying: the thought of death, or the thought of being in pain. At the mention of pain, a hundred hands immediately shoot up into the air. Indeed, our body is like a magnet attracting pain; it's part of being human, and there's no way to escape it.

Sometimes even the smallest pains feel overwhelming. A throbbing toothache can take over your whole life. A fractured bone traps your mind in its itching and aching. Even the prick of a needle can fill us with anxiety and dread. This is understandable—our entire culture looks upon pain as an enemy, and teaches us to do anything, anything to get away from it. We're wrapped up in trying to evade pain, sometimes through numbing out with addiction, sometimes through an unwholesome obsession with avoiding pain altogether.

But most of us won't be able to avoid pain forever. At some point in our lives, perhaps when we are dying, there may be great pain—and actually, pain can be our greatest teacher, once we stop frantically fleeing its presence. We need to know what to do with pain: how to see it, how to work with it. And it really helps if we can use our experiences of pain *right now* to prepare us for what's ahead.

Fifteen years ago, I was very sick and in a great deal of physical pain.

On top of this, I felt worried and discouraged because my body was sick. I dreaded having surgery, which doctors were telling me was necessary.

I was lucky; I had good friends who encouraged me to hike in the nearby mountains. Sometimes it was really a stretch for me to do this, but I gave myself that extra little push, because the mountains are my friends. They provided nourishment that made it possible for me to work with my story around my suffering.

As I gained more energy, I realized how many other women were sick just like me. I opened my heart to them and began to practice while thinking of them. My pain turned into a ransom for others. With a much more open heart, I found I was able to give myself more internal room, and to let the pain in my body just *be*. Very slowly, I gained enough courage to take care of what needed to be taken care of, and to schedule the necessary surgery.

When I think about it now, years later, I see how I was nearly caught by my suffering, hypnotized into doing nothing about my situation but worry—justifiable, perhaps, but also maybe a little self-absorbed. In Zen, we call this kind of tightness "being tied up without a rope." If I'd stayed in that place of paralysis, it would have eventually kept me from being cured. Obsessing about my illness was making me claustrophobic; changing my attitude toward the situation helped me heal. When I was able to put some breathing room around my problem, I could turn toward positive activities. And when I could accept my own sickness and ask for help, I could consider the suffering of other women in my position, and offer them my support.

Our lives include both pain and suffering. Pain is physical discomfort, while suffering is the story around pain. The Buddha said, "When touched by a feeling of pain, the ordinary uninstructed person sorrows, grieves, and laments, beats his breast, becomes distraught. So he feels two pains, physical and mental, just as if he was shot with an arrow and, right afterward, was shot with another one, so that he felt the pains of two arrows."

I had made the very human mistake of following the arrow of pain with the arrow of suffering. The first arrow, the sensation of pain, is bad enough. But it's the second arrow—the story we tell ourselves about our pain—that's the real trouble.

Liberation comes when we realize that the first arrow doesn't necessarily have to be followed by the other. Viktor Frankl wrote that everything can be taken from us but "the last of the human freedoms—to choose one's attitude in any given set of circumstances, to choose one's own way."* Can you make the distinction between the sensation of pain and the story that surrounds and amplifies it? Try saying to yourself, the next time you feel pain, "I am in pain, but I am not suffering." See if it helps to remind you not to amplify the pain by building a story around it.

Science tells us that pain is really made up of non-pain elements. We feel sensations such as duration, intensity, and cadence, and our brains do the rest, interpreting these sensations as pain and making up the story that goes along with it. But pain really has no inherent goodness or badness. It's the story we tell about pain that creates suffering. And though our frantic brains may tell us otherwise, pain changes from moment to moment, and it doesn't last forever. Even great pain is impermanent. More importantly, it is not who we really are.

If you've ever had a meditation practice based on stillness, you know that working with pain can be a path to strengthening spiritual development. Keeping your body still for many hours inevitably means you'll encounter the desire to move because you are genuinely uncomfortable. Maybe it is just a little physical irritation, a tickle in the ear, or perhaps it is a burning pain in the knee. Maybe the back is on fire or the stomach won't settle and you want to throw up. Whatever the location and scale of the pain or feeling of illness, the sensation of discomfort prompts you to move, to try to get away from it, to put distance between you and it, to find a way to resolve it as soon as possible. That's why so many meditation practices offer instructions for how to handle pain when it arrives (and why many of the practices in this book, such as *tonglen* and mindfulness, teach us how to work with pain). Pain is part of this drama of being a human, and how we approach it is essential to our living and dying.

If we explore pain as sensation made of non-pain elements, we might

* Victor E. Frankl, *Man's Search for Meaning,* trans. Ilse Lasch (Boston: Beacon Press, 1959), 9.

come to a place where we don't feel so cornered when we are in pain. Maybe we have discovered impermanence by noticing that pain is always changing in one way or another. Perhaps our pain has nourished compassion within us as we realize that many others have pain like ours. We might even look on our pain as a gift that teaches us patience, gives us the strength to endure, makes us more mindful, and reminds us that our life span is finite, our connection to life fragile. Or the raw edge of pain cuts our sanity away from us, and we are its victim. We cannot judge ourselves regarding how we respond to pain. The seemingly bravest among us may have gulped down fear in secret. Those of us most sensitive to pain might not be able to bear up for very long.

Can we have the courage to let go of our stories about pain, to experience it fully, without letting fly that second arrow of suffering? Tibetan teacher Tulku Thondup uses a wonderful image to describe what it's like when we let go of our tight grip on pain and suffering. Being free from that state, he says, is like being a skydiver, dancing in the sky even as she's falling to earth. Tulku Thondup says the trick is to relax and let go.

You're probably wondering, Fine, but how am I supposed to do that? Frankly, what has to happen is that we somehow find the courage to give up our fixed ideas—even about something as terrifying as pain. As scary as it sounds, we need to stop holding back and instead move gently forward into the arms of pain. We're afraid of being overwhelmed by it; we're afraid it will devour us. But when the pain is really great, we might feel so desperate to deal with it that our desperation generates the courage we need to meet it.

In the middle of the night, perhaps the pain of a phantom limb or womb robs you of sleep, or maybe a tumor pressing against nerves in the abdomen feels like it will consume you with its fire. At this moment, when your bravest heart steps forward and says, OK, I'm willing to experience this too, you're letting pain be your teacher.

But what do you usually do when you are in pain? Are you afraid of it? Do you try to escape it in unhealthy ways? Do you make a big deal of it? Are you likely to become anxious when faced with pain? Do you find yourself caught in the past, remembering all of your ancient pains or anticipating a pain-filled future? Or do you accept your pain, making a friend of it? Do you use pain as a way to increase your resilience, your strength? Do you take the opportunity, when in pain, to open your feelings to others who feel pain like you? Are you able to live with your pain with equanimity? Can you make your pain a teaching on impermanence and a basis for strength and compassion?

Sometimes it's skillful to take ourselves away from pain. Maybe the pain isn't worth getting involved with. We should then just let it go or ignore it. Giving it too much attention might increase it and make an unnecessary problem out of it. Or we might not have the mental or energetic resources to deal with it—we're too sensitive, too tired, or too afraid. At such times, it's usually better to focus our attention on something else, something healing, engaging, or pleasant. Distraction can be as skillful as attention when pain grows overwhelming.

When we feel stronger, have the right kind of support, or have mental buoyancy, commitment, and resilience, we may have strength to deal with pain directly and experience it fully. This can heal us, humble us, and build compassion within us. Being there for our pain may decrease the negative experience of pain as we learn about it and observe it change and as the emotions intensifying the experience of pain withdraw.

Yet sometimes we cannot transform pain through practice or psychological strategies. This is just the way it is, and we need to be realistic and sensitive to the fact that pain might be an obstacle to our practice and to our life.

Increasingly, spiritual and psychological approaches to pain management are used along with medication to enhance the effect of drugs and to help dying people relax. There are now many good medications that make it possible to manage pain effectively without diminishing awareness. I am mentioning this since I have encountered people with spiritual backgrounds who have withheld pain medication from their relatives because they believed pain was a purification process and they worried that medication would cloud the dying person's mind, or they were concerned about addiction. My approach is pretty practical and supports bringing together the gifts of modern medicine with skillful strategies of psychology and spirituality.

Wondering about this, I once asked His Holiness the Dalai Lama about what to do when pain can't be worked with through spiritual and psychological means, and he was emphatic that we should always do the best we can to help relieve pain and suffering, whether with modern pharmacology or with meditation and understanding. This was simply being compassionate, he stated. I had to agree when I thought about a close friend who was dying of pelvic cancer and who in the end requested palliative sedation. Her pain was like nothing I had ever witnessed. Nothing could touch its intensity. She bore it with both grace and fury. And in the end, it took her to her edge and over it. As she was dying, she urged her caregivers to sedate her out of her pain. There was a pause, and then a merciful assent by all those around her.

I asked His Holiness if he thought that the mind was at risk if strong drugs were used to help relieve severe pain. He said emphatically that even if medications cloud the mind, the mind-ground itself is unaffected. Untouched by conditioning or chemicals, the mind-ground is what is liberated at the moment of death. If the deceased has had a strong practice in life, then the way is clear for becoming one with the nature of mind at the moment of death, no matter what medications have been used.

Sometimes sitting with people who are in pain is pretty hard to take, like in the situation with our friend with pelvic cancer. We caregivers had to look very closely at our motivation in supporting her desire to be sedated. Was it our intolerance of suffering that was pushing the decision, or respect for our friend's need to be free of her agony? Was there any other road to take aside from the path of sedation? Could we sustain unconditional presence for her after she was sedated? Should we support her decision?

In these kinds of situations, we want so much to do something. We can feel helpless, heartbroken, angry, and confused. What really can we offer, we ask? The treasure many of us forget is our presence. Often there is nothing to do but be present for pain just as it is—or, as in the case of the friend with pelvic cancer, to support her decision to be given analgesia and then sit with her as she rode an invisible stream to her death.

Remembering our strong back and soft front, we can offer equanimity and compassion—and our ability to show up for suffering can also help the sufferer to be present. It's also important to let go of hopes and expectations for a particular outcome. And, even more, I have learned that my attachment to a so-called good outcome can actually cause more suffering.

When I visit with someone who is dying, I want to do whatever I can to relieve her pain and suffering. Sometimes, I find I can do something to help: kind words, meditation, physical touch, support for the right medical intervention, or simply bearing witness and being present. But maybe there is nothing that helps. The physical and mental misery are so great that they overwhelm all options. I need to respect the truth of this experience, accept it, be penetrated by it, be present to my own responses, and then remember that suffering and pain are transitory. If I look deeply enough, beneath the misery is an unconditioned realm where the sufferer is free of her misery. In doing this, I model the inclusive and patient qualities of heart and mind that I hope will be nurtured in this person who is suffering. Fleeing from her suffering sends the opposite message, and sadly, this is too often what happens. Fear takes over and compassion withers.

This double-arrowed vision is yet another paradox of being with dying. I try to open to both suffering and freedom from suffering. If I see only suffering, then I am caught in the relative nature of existence: we are nothing but suffering. But if I see only the pure and vast heart, then I am denying our human experience.

See if you can find fresh ways of looking at pain that make it your ally, not your enemy. Become a friend to your pain, the teachers say. Reach out to it. See what it needs; you may not know what to do, but your pain might. Give your pain space. Don't irritate it. Be a good listener to it, and try not to reject it. See what it wants to teach you. And practice, if you can, separating pain from any stories about it, so that the one arrow of pain doesn't necessarily have to be followed by a second arrow of suffering.

## MEDITATION

*Encountering Pain*

PART ONE: ATTENDING TO PAIN

In being aware of pain without adding thoughts or stories, we often find that pain transforms and even liberates itself. By working with the mind, many people discover strategies that prevent pain from reaching such an intensity that it has to be attended to with conventional medicine. One friend painted out her pain. Another set his pain to music. Another wrote out his pain. Yet if pain has reached a certain threshold, pharmaceuticals can be life-giving and profoundly supportive of a gentle death. Good medical pain management together with spiritual and psychological support can make it possible for an individual to experience active dying with fewer obstacles to the mind.

Following are several practices that have been used to transform the sharp edge of pain. First, remember why you are practicing: to help others and yourself. Let your heart open to this possibility. Then gently bring your attention to your breath. Let the breath settle down and become even and regular. Take as much time as you need.

Now bring your breath deep within your body. Gently merge your awareness with your breath as your body settles. When you breathe in, let the breath nourish you. When you breathe out, softly say the sound *ah* as though you were sighing. Continue this for at least ten breaths.

When you feel ready, bring your attention to your pain. Let yourself soften to your pain. Try to accept it without judging or fearing it. Aware of pain, breathe into it. On the out-breath, have the feeling of fully accepting your pain. Now merge your breath with your pain. Breathe into it and out from it. Breathing out, let go into whatever you are experiencing. Continue this for at least ten breaths.

With your mind, explore the sensation of pain. Is it sharp or dull, pulsating or penetrating? Is it focused or does it spread out from its source? Explore the sensation, intensity, and quality of the pain. Feel curiosity

about your exploration, not judging or fearing it, if possible. Give yourself time to really explore your pain.

Finally, gently bring your awareness to your whole body. Rest easily with
the feeling of your body. Now bring your awareness to your surroundings.
Accept whatever your experience might be. When you are ready to complete the practice, send out to others whatever good has arisen.

The following are some helpful phrases that can support your practice in
being aware of pain:

- May I find the inner resources to be open to my pain.
- May I turn toward my pain with kindness.
- May I observe my pain with equanimity.
- May I realize that this pain is not permanent.
- May I let go of my expectations around my pain.
- May I know that I am not my pain, not my body, not my illness.
- May I accept pain, knowing it does not make me bad or wrong.
- May I accept my pain, knowing that my heart is not limited by it.

## PART TWO: PAIN AND THE ELEMENTS

Be aware of your whole body and let the body settle. Accept whatever your
experience might be. Be with your body as you inhale and exhale. Consider this: Your body is composed of earth, water, fire, air, and space.

*Contemplate the element of earth.* Feel earth's solidity and strength. Now
feel the solidness of your body and the element of earth in your body. Feel
your bones, your tissue. Your body is your home. Feel welcomed by your
body. Invite your mind to feel at home in your body.

*Contemplate the element of water.* Feel water's fluidity and power to
accept anything and to purify. Feel the water element of your body: blood,
urine, mucus, generative fluid, and lymphatic fluid. Feel the sense of flow
in your body. Feel your body's power to purify. Let your mind settle and
be pure like a still pool.

*Contemplate the element of fire.* Feel fire's energy to give warmth and light, to mature and heal. Feel fire's power to transform. Feel the element of fire in your body. Be in touch with your body's warmth and its capacity to digest. Let the element of fire open up the mind to its own luminosity.

*Contemplate the element of air.* Feel the power of wind in your breath. Feel the element of air in your body. Be aware of the lightness and the strength of wind in your body. Let the element of wind bring clarity to your mind.

*Contemplate the element of space.* Feel the vastness of space. Let yourself experience the openness of your own nature. Give yourself room to experience space without limits. Let the element of space give you room for peace.

Now bring your attention to your pain. Let the element of earth give you tolerance for your pain. Let the element of water absorb your pain. Let the element of fire transform your pain. Let the element of air release your pain. Let the element of space give room for your pain.

# 9

## Giving No Fear
### *Transforming Poison into Medicine*

WHY DO WE ever follow the first arrow of pain with that second arrow of suffering? We saw how suffering and pain are different, and that one is a story about the other; but if suffering keeps arising—and it certainly seems to—then what is it that drives the stories of our misery and sorrow?

The Tibetan Wheel of Life offers a colorful folk image that illustrates how we get caught in the clutches of our various mental traps. In the nasty, fingernailed grasp of the Lord of Death, a wheel goes around and around. And at the wheel's center, propelling its axle, are three animals: a rooster, representing greed; a snake, which stands for anger; and a pig, which represents ignorance. In Buddhism, greed, hatred, and delusion are called the three poisons, and Buddha taught that it's precisely these three self-involved states that feed our suffering.

Out of his own direct experience, the Buddha saw that a hungry, hateful, or confused mind has little or no sense of connection with other beings. This kind of mind is out for itself, involved with itself, and caught in the trap of narcissism, preferences, and self-references. He also realized that our firm belief in our own identity drives us to try to change or fix the beings and things around us, creating an attitude of possessiveness, a realm of possessions, and a mind possessed by its separateness and sense of specialness. This is the stuff that makes dying hard, caregiving tiring, and grieving prolonged. If the roots of suffering are the three poisons of passion, aggression, and ignorance, then suffering's taproot is our experience of fear—a fear based in the need to preserve our sense of a fixed and separate identity.

We ask then, can we really end suffering? Is there a path, a way, that can help us change our poisons into the medicines of generosity, clarity, and fearlessness? How can we develop mercy and taste boundlessness and the ease of freedom, even in the presence of death? I once heard a Tibetan teacher say that suffering also has beneficial qualities: it can nourish our longing for freedom. Then he went on to say that our compassion is ignited when we are in the presence of the suffering of others.

By being with his own suffering, the Buddha learned how to transform it, ultimately awakening to what is real, what is true. He did not avoid his own misery or that of others. He saw that in the mess of our misery many gifts may be discovered, including the gift of mercy. Suffering brought him closer to the heart of his spiritual life, and suffering led him to freedom.

An old joke goes, "Religion is for people who are afraid of hell; spirituality is for people who have been through hell." Buddha went through hell. Most of us have been through some version of the underworld, and strangely enough, we are usually better off for having gone through these difficulties. Even complexity theory illustrates this truth—living systems become more robust when they break down and then learn how to repair themselves. You and I are more robust for the challenges we have faced. But it takes a lot of courage to flail and fail, courage to let go into not-knowing, and to let go of our attachment to a good outcome. And this is particularly challenging if we are caregivers. We are there to help. So how do we both help and let go of any gain?

I think it is important to remember that the Buddha was simply a man who looked directly at suffering and death and let these two guide him to a more meaningful and merciful life. Others have done the same. The Buddha seems to have been a very brave human being. We can be brave, too. What he went through is not so far from what you and I have experienced in our own lives.

Had the Buddha been a god or divine or filled with inherent knowledge or completely blessed, he probably would not have left home and embarked on his difficult spiritual search. Like many of us, he pursued a quest for meaning and awakening, and in the course of it, he suffered even more. He sat in the fire, and like the metal of a fine sword, was strengthened through the encounter with elemental energies.

Aware of his own suffering and the suffering of others, he realized that it is essential to be in touch with the truth that there is suffering in this life; he also saw that there is a way through suffering, and one can be free of suffering. He saw this from the perspective of having confronted his difficulties, not having fled from them. It seems that maturation is not an easy process for most of us, not even for a Buddha.

And yes, suffering is a sword that cuts both ways: it can free us or send us into hiding. Whether we are dying, caring, or grieving, if we run from suffering to nowhere or into addiction—be it hyperactivity, drugs, food, sex, shopping, or even sleep—we will only be driven into deeper confusion, making it all the more difficult to see what's really going on. This is why we step out of the rush of our lives periodically, to remember who we really are. Stopping to investigate the mind and heart is essential in our work of caregiving and in being with dying.

There exists a basic mind-state that is free from all dualities and that excludes nothing. This mental experience brings into our perception the presence of our true nature: Buddha-nature, Christ-nature, the great heart that is beyond all sorrow. Buddhism teaches that this basic nature of our mind is pure and bright. When we die, this is what is first liberated into the clear light of death.

From the perspective of many wisdom traditions, death is seen as the ultimate moment for the complete liberation of the mind from all entanglements, all sorrows, all separateness. If we look really deeply, we may see that suffering and freedom from suffering are embedded in each other. In the apparent darkness of death rests the light of freedom, if only we can perceive it. Our practice and our very lives are also where we can see the light of freedom.

Imagine sitting with a dying person, someone in intractable pain; or maybe you are that person: a person in intense discomfort, a dying person. Imagine really letting yourself open to what feelings might be present in this situation. Now, look through the pain to the deep ground of being, that unshakable heart where all categories, dualities, cravings, delusions and dislikes have never been. See your or her true nature, free from all pain—and at the same time, be present with the truth of suffering.

Can we see two things at one and the same moment, like seeing that the wave and water are not separate? Maybe, even if we can't feel the truth of it right now, we can have faith that this is so. When we are caught in the tight grip of unhappiness, this is often hard to do. We can help ourselves by remembering what we have understood from teachings, reading, or our deepest insights. Remembering the truth when you cannot experience it in the present moment can be a lifeline tying us close to our open heart.

Another way you can begin to see with nondualistic vision is to consider your own life. You exist only through a vast web of interconnectedness. There are your ancestors and your parents; then all your relationships, from your family and community to the food you eat and the air you breathe. You are in relationship with literally everything in the phenomenal world, in the past, in the present, and even in the future.

You are nonduality itself because of this boundless, endless net that weaves through all of your life and the lives of all beings and things. Everything that happens in your life happens because of the reality of interconnectedness. You and I have no real separate and inherent self. We exist only through our connections with every single thing. And in the same way, we also can't separate life from death or suffering from freedom.

Even though we might be able to figure this out logically, we must taste the experience of liberation ourselves to make this truth real. The Buddha knew that suffering could not be transformed by telling someone how to do it. He himself sat down under a tree for a long time, and vowed not to leave that spot till he saw the truth. He was determined and committed.

Realization comes about through direct experience. Since most of us haven't savored real freedom just yet, it is important to have faith that freedom from suffering is possible. Faith like this is not an idea but an experience. It is a kind of bright longing from some place deep inside of ourselves that senses the mystery of boundlessness. Faith helps us to stop and look deeply.

I remember the first time I read Leo Tolstoy's novella *The Death of Ivan Ilyich.*\* I had faith in Tolstoy's words, and that faith forced me to stop and look more deeply into my own experience and into my mind. The ending of the novella depicts an unexpected liberation at the moment of death. Tolstoy's wretched protagonist Ivan moves slowly toward his death in a state of depression and denial. His family is unhappy and distant, and he himself doesn't seem to have a clue. Just on the threshold of death, Ivan appears to everyone around him to be in a state of utter misery. But Ivan is actually having realization after realization.

First he drops out of his experience of pain; pain falls away, and he realizes: there is no pain. Then he drops through the door of death only to realize: there is no death. To the wonder of the reader, at the deathless deathpoint he becomes one with that clear light. "What joy!" he exclaims inwardly, just as someone at his bedside says, "It is finished."

When I sit with a dying person, or someone caught in the tight fist of pain or suffering, I might hope that he will be free of pain and suffering, live longer, and die well; or I might fear the possibility of future pain and suffering he may have to endure. Then I have to stop, give myself some time and space to let go of my hopes, and then reconsider. I wish the best for him, and I will do my best for him, and I also remember that death is inevitable, and perhaps for my patient, like Ivan Ilyich proclaimed, there is no pain, there is no death. I really can't know. I then sit with the two truths: the truth of suffering and the truth of freedom from suffering. And I try to be open to what "wants" to happen.

I also watch my priorities shift as I consider the preciousness of life at this moment. I consider what is really important to do or not do in this particular situation. I do not reject suffering, mine or that of another, for it brings many things to me, from compassion to a sense of immediacy. Also faith in basic goodness is the raft that carries me over the waters of

---

\* Leo Tolstoy, *The Death of Ivan Ilyich and Other Stories* (New York: Penguin, 1960).

misery. This faith brings me back again and again to the boundless shore of not-knowing.

I once sat for many hours with a friend dying of cancer. She had been sick for years, and the cancer had eaten into her abdominal area. This was a strong experience for me. There were times when the smell from her body was so pungent that it was difficult for people to come into her room.

This woman was unfailingly kind to her visitors, always asking, "How are you? Do you need anything?" Particularly toward the end of her days, when the thread tying her to life was so thin that it frayed with each breath, sitting in that room with her body unbinding, her breath uneven, her skin a coppery yellow, I felt the whole world present. Everything was there; nothing was left out. Her good works were there, and her anger and anguish as well. The suffering of many women was there, and so was the courage and compassion of women. Fear was present and so was fearlessness.

Suffering can give birth to a bigger perspective and greater resilience, and, strangely enough, suffering is the mother of kindness and compassion if we turn toward it with openness, making a friend of it. Suffering wrings us out, leaving the weave of our life more open. In this openness, we often can be with suffering in a bigger, kinder, and more tender way. Suffering is also the kindling that ignites compassion. This all might unfold as slowly as geological time or be like a flash of lightning. However, compassion, kindness, altruistic joy, and equanimity are already within us. Our circumstances awaken them in their own time.

In Plato's *Phaedo*, Socrates said, "True philosophers make death and dying their profession." I think our Greek meant that we should practice dying with every breath, and study dying in our every moment. I also think that the terrible squeezing of the heart we feel when first facing the unknown is the moment when our horizon begins to expand past the bounds of suffering. Just one person seeing both the sorrow and at the same time the great heart of who we really are can open shuttered eyes and let the light shine out even before the moment of death.

Up until the day before my father died, he told us the truth with his dry humor. One morning as I was sitting with him, he said, "Well, kid, it looks like I'm going to die." I reached over, put my hand on his, and said quietly,

"I think you're right." As I looked into his blue eyes, I watched a wave of apprehension pass through him. Then he punned, "Well, it's about time." We smiled at each other as each saw the truth in what the other had said. Then we sat together in silence for the rest of the morning, his eyes filled with peace and mine with gratitude.

In the end, my father was not afraid to die. He was a brave and realistic person, a person with natural spirituality guiding him. As he grew older and nearing death, peace of mind graced his days. He did not cling to any illusion of solidity. He did not resist the many reminders of his own impermanence, nor did he insulate himself from truth by hoping for a particular outcome.

Three days before he died, he reviewed his life with his children and grandchildren. It was not an easy task as his review included terrible experiences he had gone through in World War II. After his disclosures, he seemed to let go and relax into groundlessness. He had faced his suffering, and then he moved past what was already behind him to the road taking him toward the destination we call death.

Suffering usually pushes us onto the spiritual path. Often it takes an accident, a catastrophic diagnosis, a disaster, or great loss for us to break open. Then, when we begin to explore the truth of suffering, we often find within each poison the nectar of wisdom, kindness, and love. But we must first discard the belief that we can make our suffering go away. Instead, we learn to stay with it. Then we become curious about it. This is a fundamental change of attitude: we accept our suffering and determine to help ourselves by investigating its cause. We are forced to lie down in what the poet Yeats called "the foul rag-and-bone shop of the heart."* This is where most of us begin our journey home—among the rags and bones of our tender and awful brokenness.

The following practice of *tonglen,* or giving and receiving, develops our ability to be with dying, suffering, and to open to the vastness of our

---

* William Butler Yeats, from "The Circus Animal's Desertion," in *The Collected Poems of W. B. Yeats* (Hertfordshire, U.K.: Wordsworth Editions, 2000), 297.

original nature. The great kindness of this rare practice releases our whole being to suffering's overwhelming presence, cultivates our strength and willingness to transform alienation into compassion, and is one of the richest and bravest practices we can do. This one technique has helped countless dying people, family and professional caregivers attend to their own fears around pain, dying, and loss, and has given them a real basis for the joining of compassion and equanimity. This is one of the great meditation jewels that offers a way to nurture the natural energy of mercy and basic goodness.

We may discover that when we rest in basic goodness, ignorance and confusion are just the other side of the coin of not-knowing. When we stop directing aggression toward others or ourselves, the sharpness of anger enables us to look without fear at things as they are. And letting go of our desire for the four traps of confirmation, comfort, consolation, and security, then longing transforms into a commitment to engage with the world. This is truly giving no fear.

## MEDITATION

### Giving and Receiving through Tonglen

To begin the practice, sit in meditation posture, relax in a chair, or lie down, however you can be relaxed and open. Gently close your eyes and let your body and mind settle. You can say the following prayer to help prepare you for the practice:

> Having recognized the futility of my selfishness and the great
> benefit of loving others, may I bring all beings to joy. May I send
> all my virtues and happiness to others through the strength of
> my practice, and may I receive the suffering and difficulties of
> all beings in all realms.

Begin by breathing in whatever you are feeling—fear, agitation, anger, resistance. On the exhalation, accept whatever is present for you in this moment, giving it space to just be. Do this breath practice until you are calm and alert.

When you feel settled, begin the second stage of the practice, which is establishing a rhythm of breathing. On your in-breath imagine that you are inhaling heavy, hot air. On your out-breath visualize exhaling cool, light air. Continue with this pattern—breathing in heaviness and breathing out lightness—until it is familiar. The heaviness is suffering; the lightness is well-being. Then go further and imagine that you are breathing through all the pores of your body. On the in-breath heavy, hot air enters every pore. On the out-breath, cool light flows from every pore.

Now visualize a metal sheath around your heart. This metal sheath is everything about you that is difficult for you to accept: your self-importance, selfishness, self-cherishing, self-pity. It is the band of fear that hardens your heart.

Tonglen invites you to dissolve this sheath and open your heart to its natural nonjudgmental state of warmth, kindness, and spaciousness. You can do this by visualizing the metal breaking apart when the in-breath of suffering touches it. When the heart opens, the hot, heavy air vanishes into its vast space. What arises is natural mercy. It is this quality of unarmored heart that allows you to be with suffering and at the same time to see beneath the suffering.

Bring to your mind some being, dead or alive, with whom you feel a deep connection: a parent, child, pet, your grandmother, your dearest friend, your beloved teacher—someone who is suffering. You would do anything to help this person. Be with her and feel what she is experiencing. Let your whole being turn toward her suffering and your wish that it might be relieved. See how vulnerable she is. Like a mother who will do anything to help her child, you will do anything to help your friend.

Visualize the suffering of your beloved as polluted, hot smoke and breathe it in through your whole body. The instant that the in-breath of suffering touches the metal sheath of self-centeredness around your heart, the sheath breaks apart, and your heart opens. The hot smoke instantly vanishes into the great space of your heart, and from this space spontaneously arises an out-breath of mercy and healing. Send a deep, cool, light, and spacious healing breath to your friend. Let the out-breath flow through every pore of your body.

Let your loved one's suffering remind you of the many others who find themselves suffering in the same way. This friend is your connection to them. Breathe in the suffering. Let your heart break open. Send this person healing with your out-breath.

To bring the practice to your own life, remember a time when you were in a difficult situation. You may still hold energy around this difficulty. You may have been hurt, angry, depressed, outraged, or afraid. Remembering the feeling as vividly as possible, breathe it in as hot, heavy, polluted smoke. Let go of any sense of blame, any object of blame. Don't be involved with the story. Rather, breathe in the raw feeling directly as the hot smoke of suffering. Take it in through every pore of your body. Own the heat and rawness of it completely.

This practice takes a lot of courage. You might find yourself resisting breathing in the suffering. If so, you can breathe in your resistance. You can breathe in alienation, piety, boredom, arrogance, confusion, grief, or clinging—whatever flavor your suffering of the moment takes. Breathe out the sense of spaciousness, kindness, and surrender that arises. Shower these qualities on yourself in a rain of cool, healing light. Aerating your suffering threatens the ego—that small, tight self that habitually clings to anger, blame, or shame as a way of fortifying its illusion of solidity and separateness. Don't analyze what you are doing. Don't try to figure it out. Don't justify it. Simply do the practice. Breathe in the hot smoke of your suffering and breathe out sympathetic space. As you breathe in your tarlike suffering, own it completely. Then breathe out clarity and surrender, relief and kindness.

Now imagine sitting with someone who is dying. See her as clearly as you can. You are sitting quietly and peacefully next to her, following her breath. You see that she is in pain. You can almost feel her pain. Visualize the sheath of fear around your heart, that tough membrane you use to protect yourself from the world. Breathe in her pain as hot, grimy smoke, through every pore in your body. Let your heart break open to her pain.

Now release the pain completely as you breathe out kindness, giving her all the good you have known in your life.

Now imagine that this person who is dying is you. See yourself in a hospital bed. Your body feels tired and heavy. You might be fearful. Breathe in that fear as hot smoke. Let it dissolve the tightness around your heart. Feel your heart open to its natural greatness. Then let go of your breath completely as you send all the good in your heart to the world.

Imagine that this is the moment of your death. Let your heart completely relax and open like a flower as you let go of your last breath, giving the great merit of your life to all beings everywhere. Dissolve the visualization and rest your body and mind in openness and gratitude.

# 10

## Take Care of Your Life, Take Care of the World
### *Seeing My Own Limits with Compassion*

IN BEING with dying, as in the boundless abodes, we're asked to offer loving-kindness not only to those with whom we work, but also to *ourselves*. Just as a mother can care best for her child after her own needs have been met, it's crucial that we recognize our own limits with compassion—in the same way that, in an airplane crisis, we're instructed to place the oxygen mask over our own face first before we try to help those around us.

Keeping your personal life together is not an optional indulgence but an absolute necessity when it comes to being of use to others in the world. We aren't separate from everything else; when we suffer, others suffer. Our well-being *is* the well-being of others. So make time to connect with your heart, for as the Zen saying goes, "If you take care of your mind, you take care of the world."

When you have not seen the light of day in a month except for the short walk between your house and your car, when you find dishes in the sink from last week and laundry in a mountainous pile, *stop*. Take a time-out. Clean up the messes, bring order to the chaos around you, and consider what you can do to bring things back into balance. Especially when working with the dying, you need your home to be a refuge, a place in which to rest and restore yourself, a sanctuary in which you can be nourished and safe. If you try to cut corners by ignoring your personal or domestic needs, you might eventually pay with your sanity and health.

In addition to your literal home, another precious place to take refuge is within a contemplative practice. Without this inner home—an uncluttered place into which we can retreat and close the door for a time on all the dramas around and within us—our lives will be limited by the conditioning that drives us, without our even knowing it. A spiritual practice offers a concentrated, still place in which to cultivate calmness and kindness toward ourselves and others, and can bring insight as well as refreshment.

Here are a few good principles for self-care:

- See your limits with compassion.
- Set up a schedule that is sane.
- Know what practices and activities refresh you, and make time for them.
- Actively involve, include, and support other caregivers.
- Develop a plan for doing your work in a way that is mindful, restorative, wholesome, and healthy.

I once worked with a hospice nurse who had a hard time taking care of herself. After we talked, I suggested she direct loving-kindness to those parts of her life that felt the most worthless. This was difficult for her precisely because she felt so undeserving, but finally she agreed to practice with the phrase "I turn toward my suffering with kindness." When we feel psychologically impoverished, it's initially not easy for us to take care of ourselves. But after a while, she felt able to add, "May I be happy." So she practiced breathing in and breathing out while saying these phrases to herself—in the morning on waking, while she drove to her hospice job, as she walked from one patient's room to another's, while falling asleep at night.

Slowly, as she became comfortable with sending herself kindness, she began to say these phrases to herself while actually working with patients. And eventually, she felt ready to turn her heart and mind toward those with whom she worked, sending *them* loving-kindness. But long before that became possible, without any conscious effort on her part, her spirit naturally began to brighten. Her love and concern for her patients arose from a more genuine place, one that was well rested and brimming with self-respect. Her faithful practice of self-care led directly to her increased availability as a caregiver.

All of the world's spiritual traditions share a belief in the importance of non-harming. Yet we often forget that non-harming doesn't just apply to others, but to ourselves as well. You harm yourself when you neglect your own needs, and you create harm for yourself in hurting others through your self-neglect. If we really value this precious human life each of us has been given, then we will take care of it, helping others indirectly just as much as through direct service.

A physician I knew turned his attention to practicing self-care only when he found himself passing through a long valley of depression. When he started gaining weight, having difficulties sleeping, and looking out at the world with eyes of despair, he wondered what to do. He felt trapped in a dry, gray, dusty corner of his mind, and began to think he didn't deserve to care for others any longer. He admitted to me, with great honesty, that he could barely tolerate his patients and saw them as a burden. He had worked too hard, seen too much suffering, cared too little for himself, and had a big dose of compassion fatigue. Yet even in this emotionally desolate place, he somehow knew his pain wasn't permanent. He wisely recognized sadness and fatigue for what they were: invitations to slow down, to give more attention to his life. He cleared his calendar and, in spite of his painful inertia and busy schedule, made himself go on a two-week hiking trip in the mountains of southern Colorado.

One evening at sunset, in the blue and red dusk of the San Juans, he suddenly began to cry. He had never mourned the death of his own father, or wept for the many patients he had lost. The precious road of grief opened for him in those mountains. Face wet with tears, he vowed to give himself the necessary time to turn toward the well of sorrow—the only way, ultimately, he would be able to retrieve his heart of compassion.

Too many professional caregivers experience burnout when their medical institutions push them. You often see professional caregivers being financially rewarded for working overtime or taking on the night shift. And this kind of overwork inevitably results in the very numbness that makes it almost impossible to perceive an institution's dysfunctional work demands and expectations. Stress, exhaustion, and numbness become a vicious cycle in which both caregivers and patients—and ultimately, institutions themselves—suffer.

Caregivers also burn out when they believe they don't do enough for their clients and overcompensate in response. A hospice worker who loses a patient may feel so guilty that he redoubles his efforts on behalf of all his other clients. When such fear and guilt drive our urge to serve, they have the power to destroy us. Over the years I have met far too many former health-care professionals who have left their jobs because they don't know how to break the cycle of overwork or they are burned out by secondary trauma. They were simply used up. Most of us only realize our limits once we have gone far past them; a professional caregiver may already be dangerously fatigued or ill herself by the time she realizes she's used up. At that point, leaving caregiving altogether is often the only solution.

Family caregivers, too, suffer burnout just like professionals. The same fear and guilt, added to inadequate financial resources or community support, can tip the balance for a caregiver who may already feel unbearably alone in caring for her loved one, and can lead her to depression, anger, despair, and even abuse or neglect of the dying one. But if caregivers find ways to respect their own limits, acknowledging them with compassion and sensitivity, they can offer powerful and loving assistance in the right proportion to their own priorities.

I was very impressed when I observed Michelle helping take care of a man who was dying of AIDS and needed both physical and spiritual support. Michelle spent several hours a day looking after some of his basic needs, including cooking and cleaning, bathing him, and making sure he took his meds. His partner also had AIDS but was not as ill.

Each morning when Michelle arrived, she brought a sense of order into the house. She did the simplest things easily and quietly. When the practical tasks were attended to, she would sit with the couple and listen to them talk about their concerns. Then the three of them would spend time together just being quiet. Occasionally, I too was there during these quiet times. The house was clean and peaceful, and the four of us would sit on the bed or near the sick man while he rested. No one felt the need to do anything, including talk. After a while Michelle would leave, slipping out of the room without a goodbye.

One day I asked Michelle how she took care of herself. She said that, first of all, she never stayed longer than three hours with her friends. She had created a sane schedule, one in which others stayed with the men so that she could let go of them when it was time. She also had a daily meditation and exercise practice, and she made sure she got plenty of sleep and regular meals. Her serene, humble presence, without a doubt, contributed to the deep feeling of calm that surrounded their home.

Michelle's friend died first, very peacefully; and then it was our job to support his partner through his grief and his own dying, which followed some months later. Again, Michelle was involved in a kind and measured way. She was present for that death, along with other friends—a death as peaceful as his partner's had been. Michelle's contribution to the whole situation was profound. She helped to create an atmosphere of sustaining peacefulness that touched everyone. Her way of caring for others was simple, clear, and inspiring. And she did this by having clear boundaries and a set schedule, gathering others to help, and taking kind, compassionate care of herself.

Michelle knew herself well. She wanted to give her friends the best care possible, and she knew that this would require pacing herself, so she set up a system that worked for her friends as well as for their caregivers. In working with a dying person, it helps to establish a strategy that builds in pacing, a rhythm of care and self-care that will permit us to be fully present instead of strung out and stressed.

Like Michelle, we need a reasonable, responsible plan; without one, we can be pretty sure that self-care will probably remain low on the list of priorities. When we train professional caregivers, we ask each person to create a plan for how they will take care of themselves when they return to their jobs—and a few months later, we mail them a copy as a reminder.

One busy New York nurse created the following plan for herself, and kept a copy on her fridge at home and in her mailbox at work so she could review it regularly:

> *Body:* Stretch fifteen minutes in the morning on rising and in the evening before bed. One-hour yoga class on my day off. Fast walking to and from work twice a week. Dance aerobics class every two weeks. Less junk food! Eat mindfully. Eat healthy foods on a regular schedule of meals and snacks. Take daily vitamin supplements.

> *Mind:* Cut down on TV and morning newspaper. Read more in the fields of psychology, philosophy, spirituality, complementary therapies. Look into holistic nursing. Go to a museum and read a really good book at least once a month.

> *Spirit:* Investigate mindfulness-based stress reduction program. Sit quietly after morning and evening stretching. Find a meditation group and participate at least twice a month. Practice walking meditation and sitting with patients. Go on retreat once a year. Explore all this with colleagues.

> *Psyche:* Continue therapy. Start a nurse support group addressing grief and burnout.

> *Social:* Have more fun!

Of course, your own self-care plan will be different, depending on your personality, needs, and circumstances; maybe you need more snacks and less reading. My own experience has been that regular vigorous exercise and a strong meditation practice are absolutely essential for grounding and stabilizing our energy, especially when we feel fatigued or vulnerable. But the point is to have a plan that will work for *you,* incorporating islands of care and nourishment throughout your life. Find ways to remind yourself to do these things for yourself, and learn to forgive yourself when you fail to remember.

A social worker wrote me the following note after the Being with Dying professional training program:

> One of the messages I got from our meeting was to focus more on my own contemplative life, so I've been building a solid and dependable meditation practice . . . powerfully simple and helpful. I've also been attending the palliative care service at my hospital, and daily I practice the art of straight talk and silence.

I also highly recommend working with a partner. We all need support and feedback, but too many caregivers find themselves working alone even within a team. Working in twos makes it possible to offer a richer and more flexible kind of support. Coworkers can support each other during complex situations, evaluate each other's work and make constructive suggestions.

The more peaceful and accepting caregivers are, the more helpful we can be to dying people. So recognize your limits with compassion; share your joy, stability, strength, openness, and humor; help to create a strong, supportive community; and above all, don't neglect the practice of self-care. If you really want to take care of the whole world, start by taking care of your life.

## MEDITATION

### Boundless Caring

Bringing together the strength of equanimity and the tenderness of compassion, the courage of presence and the openness of surrender, the following practices can nourish healthy caregiving practice as we offer our lives to the well-being of others. In the experience of giving care, there is a delicate balance between opening our heart endlessly (compassion) and accepting the limits of what we can do and how we and others feel (equanimity). Most of us need to cultivate this balance between compassion—the tenderness of the heart in response to suffering—and equanimity—

the spacious stillness that accepts things as they are. The balance of compassion and equanimity allows us to care without becoming overwhelmed and unable to cope because of that caring.

The phrases we use reflect this balance. Choose phrases that are personally meaningful to you. Remember to find as comfortable a position as possible, and to take a few deep, soft breaths in order to let your body settle. Bring your attention to your breath and silently repeat your chosen phrase.

- May my love for others flow boundlessly.
- May the power of loving-kindness sustain me.
- May I find the inner resources to truly be able to give.
- May I remain in peace and let go of expectations.
- May I offer my care and presence unconditionally, knowing it may be met by gratitude, indifference, anger, or anguish.
- May I offer love, knowing that I cannot control the course of life, suffering, or death.
- May I see my limits compassionately, just as I view the suffering of others.
- May I accept things as they are.

# 11

## The Jeweled Net
### *Communities of Care*

I N OUR modern culture of isolation, disconnected from one another and from ourselves, we can easily forget that in the past, death took place in a social context. As a rite of passage that happens within a community, the experience of dying usually involved an entire extended family and a village.

Today, often those who give care believe they are the only ones available to help, even though others may have wanted to participate but felt chased away. A student of mine watched aghast as his mother, the primary caregiver for his dying grandfather, systematically cut off all sources of outside help and then insisted that she had no other choice but to take care of her father alone. Her actions, seemingly so heroic, predictably led to compassion fatigue. Eventually, my student's burned-out mother became verbally abusive to her increasingly helpless and confused father. Both dying person and caregivers will suffer less if they accept the fact that creating a network of people to participate in the process of dying is the only sustainable, healthy way to provide long-term support for everyone.

The metaphor of the jeweled net gives us some sense of how a community of caregivers can function. At each node in the net, we find a jewel, a being who cares; each caregiver reflects the shared concern and compassion of all other caregivers. In the Buddhist Avatamsaka Sutra, the question is asked, how can all these jewels be considered one jewel? If we now arbitrarily select one of these jewels for inspection and look closely at it, we will discover that in its polished surface there are reflected all the other jewels in the net, infinite in number. Not only that, but each of the jewels reflected in this one jewel is also reflecting all the other jewels, so that there is an infinite reflecting process occurring. This is a wonderful image exemplifying interconnectedness.

Instead of isolating ourselves, can we share the responsibilities of giving care? Can we find creative ways to bring the entire community into the experience of care, educating them if necessary? Can we make space so that all those who want to serve can do so? Can we share our compassion reflectively and supportively?

French philosopher Simone Weil defined fellowship and community as being made up of those who ask one another, "What are you going through?"* This expression of human-to-human concern is an example of the sharing of affection and kindness that holds our families and communities together. Another related question to ask: "For whom does this matter?" Often, community members will surround a dying person spontaneously, from those who give direct care to those who simply care.

In being with dying, one of the first helpful things to do is to take stock and identify the community, including patient, family, friends, pets, volunteers and professional caregivers, the postman, and the pharmacist. Who are those who want to know what others are going through? Who are those that care? For whom does this death matter?

## THE IMPORTANCE OF COMMUNITY

I don't think we can sanely do the work of being with dying outside of some form of community. You may have heard the phrase "relationship-centered care" used to describe one model for caregiving, a model based in a strong vision of extended community. So many kinds of relationships around a dying person make a difference—the relationships between the

---

* Simone Weil, "The Love of God and Affliction," in *Waiting for God,* trans. Emma Craufurd (New York: G. P. Putnam's Sons, 1951), 64.

dying person and her health care professional; between her friends and family and the medical team; between the health care professionals themselves; among family, friends, and volunteers; between all the community members and the dying person; between dying people in a support group; and between a dying person and her beloved pet.

Coordinating all these diverse relationships seems like an impossibly intimidating job for any overwhelmed family member, busy RN, or part-time volunteer. Yet it can be helpful to have a rough map of those who give care, because often it is in the cracks between these complex relationships that the support system around the dying person breaks down. Developing community is important work, and community is a great resource too often neglected. I have seen some pretty sorry mishaps around dying people because relationships were not recognized, understood, or tended.

The caregiving community offers many different types of support, from the outer circle around the dying person to the very center. We need to be aware of who cares, how they care, and how they feel about caring. Find a working structure that provides support for all caregivers; build trust in individual caregivers as well as in the caregiving team or family. Be tolerant of differences in caregiving styles—there is no one right way to take care of a dying person, and most of us do the very best we can.

## TIMELY RESPITE IS KEY

Look for ways to make time off for close family and caregivers. I knew a man whose wife was ill for years. When I met him, he had not taken a day for himself in many months. Shortly before her death, the husband didn't seem to like his dying wife very much, nor did he like himself. He felt resentful, obligated, and afraid of his anger. To make matters more complicated, he had begun a sexual relationship with a coworker. This relationship seemed to give him relief from the years he had spent taking care of his wife, but he was guilty and withdrawn as his wife approached active dying. His attempt to "save and serve" his wife had led him far afield.

The house was full of conflicting behaviors and feelings, from love to hate, from peace to agitation. As caregivers, my colleagues and I found ourselves in the midst of all this confusion. Difficult circumstances were the ingredients we were given.

In working with her family, I was reminded that caregivers need to keep themselves strong and fresh for what is often a convoluted journey into death. For this family, we gave her husband a pause from caregiving, and the dying woman support as she called for her last and most extreme medical intervention. The five of us involved felt we had arrived on the scene a little late, however. The damage to her feelings was evident, and our patient died a pretty hard death. This we had to accept. Raw anger and confusion had overwhelmed fifteen people in the family network, and our job was to draw the network together for the concluding act in a difficult drama. As the family members went through their changes in regard to one another, they also went through dramatic shifts in their attitude toward us, from love to hate and back again. Later, the husband told me he wished he had sought respite, not sexual relief. That was his conclusion as he was dealing with the complexities of his grief.

## Caregiver as Angel and Demon

Caregivers often learn their most valuable lessons when a dying person and his family and friends perceive them in ways that are unrealistic. The caregiver can appear like a guardian angel one minute and a demon the next. To complicate matters, caregivers can also find themselves in tangled emotional relationships with family members or the dying person. It is easy to take personally a family or dying person's affection, criticism, or anger. Many of us have been hurt by those whom we are taking care of. We have also been hurt by our colleagues or family members. Most of us will find ourselves preferring one person to another. And of course, we are not always skillful and can hurt others.

## The Work of Discovery

If you're a caregiver, it helps to embrace not-knowing, staying open and learning how to help even when you aren't sure of exactly the right thing to do. Your work is the work of discovery, of helping to uncover the rich spiritual basis of each person's life and the life of the community, and supporting and strengthening the opening of faith for all. And don't think your work is just with the dying person—if your meditation practice has matured, your own strength and kindness can be a model of inherent strength and kindness for others. Like the sympathetic string on a sitar, you can awaken these qualities in another simply by being genuinely kind and aware yourself. It is not what we do but how we are that makes it possible for another to discover their own natural compassion and openness toward suffering and the unknown.

And while a caregiver can bear witness to the suffering of another and might inspire the sufferer to bear witness to his or her own misery, just as often the dying one can bear witness to a caregiver's confusion and doubt and inspire confidence, ease, and acceptance in the one who is giving care. Whichever role we find ourselves playing, we do well to nurture trust so that the knot in the weave of things can be opened to reveal its intricacy. Whether we are actively dying or are giving care, we find ourselves humbled and enriched by being fully present to the unacceptable, the unexplained, the unjustified, and the unknowable. Rather than seeing dying and death as problems to be solved or overcome, we can begin to regard dying as an experience rich in meaning and value, a developmental phase in our maturation process, and even a preparation for deathless enlightenment.

When Ann, herself a brilliant young doctor, was diagnosed with an extremely malignant, fast-moving form of brain cancer, she found herself at the center of a large and diverse support community. Other physicians, highly educated family members and medical research colleagues, along with spiritual teachers, healers, and artists all had strong opinions about Ann's treatment and her choices regarding orthodox versus alternative medicine. She herself had specialized in unconventional health practices. Amid all the intensity, Ann and her husband held open the dialogue between the two worlds while creating space for Ann to make her own decisions.

When I walked into their home two months before Ann died, I was amazed by the flood of advice, information, and people; I can only imagine how she felt. Folks had arrived on her doorstep to heal her. People all over the world were praying for her. Her friends and family researched every kind of special diet and alternative therapy. The country's top specialists offered their recommendations via e-mail. This one and that one were convinced they had the right solution for her. Others stated emphatically that there was no cure for her aggressive brain tumor. Witnessing this rich gathering of individuals, I wondered how Ann and her husband would find their way through the complexity of differences.

Fortunately, Ann was not only a gifted physician, she had a kind, firm hand when it came to dealing with diametrically opposed opinions in her community. For his part, her husband supported her with goodwill and humor. Surrounded by a torrent of information and opinions, the two did what was typical of them: they kept the lines of communication clear and active, opened themselves willingly to all possibilities, and finally relied on their intuition, intelligence, and good hearts to make the necessary decisions. Using their skills and patience, they managed to bring together this potentially discordant group into a flexible net of support, involving almost everyone in the community of compassion without distancing anyone who wanted to help.

In the end, though, it was Ann who decided to go see the healer—and it was she who chose not to follow his advice when he told her to put aside traditional medical interventions. It was her call to have radiation—and her call to stop. Cradled in a mandala of care, Ann took the lead in her own dying.

Around the time Ann became ill, I was sitting with Kyogen's koan about the man in a tree. Koans are traditional Zen teaching stories used to deepen practice, and this particular one describes a monk who's just barely hanging on to a tree branch—by his teeth. According to the koan, he can't reach the branch to grasp it with his hands, and his feet can't touch the tree's trunk to support his weight. Just then, someone passes underneath and asks him a question about Buddhism. Great timing! If the monk doesn't answer, he's falling down on the job by not meeting the questioner's spiritual need. But if he does answer, he falls down, period. What should he do?

This wild-sounding koan is really about the dilemma of our life. We are always caught between a rock and a hard place, damned if we do and damned if we don't. But the deeper problem is that we keep looking for "solutions." Sitting with Ann, I felt like the monk in the tree. There was no solution to her sickness and suffering; there were no answers. Although many in her community felt they knew the "right" thing to do, I didn't know who among all these friends and advisers was right—or even whether anyone was. I could only hang from the branch by my teeth, knowing that even to look for a solution was an admission of blind hope, and in such a complex community, it might help if at least one person rests with "beginner's mind." As long as I had hope, I would find myself approaching the situation with stale logic and fixed ideas about how some other experience would be better than just living through the time we had left together. Thus I found myself hanging free in sublime defeat.

So with Ann, her husband, and their community, I tried to stay present, flowing with the waters of change. In the end there was little to do but bear witness, listening to them and their friends as they sorted through questions and options. They themselves were the best caregivers they could have, with their good motivation, intelligence, and courage to face whatever was arising.

From this experience, as from many others, I keep learning to accept things as they are, whether the truth of suffering or differing views and beliefs about sickness and dying. In the final analysis, it probably won't be our faith or beliefs that guide the dying person and the community, so we may as well let go of trying to be right. The caregiver is just the man hanging in the tree, being with the impossible where there is no solution. And if we are lucky, the whole community is hanging there with us.

## MEDITATION

### The Circle of Truth

One very skillful way in which a community can come together and share their experiences is in the practice of council. Dedicated to speaking honestly and constructively, and listening without prejudice, council's circle of truth gives us a chance to communicate about the deepest issues of our lives.

Council does not necessarily lead us into seeing things the same way. It is not a consensus process. Rather, we recognize that each individual has his or her own wisdom. When differing views and experiences are expressed, we discover the richness of differences and diversity. Dying people can hear the perspectives of caregivers, and vice versa. One person with AIDS who sat in council with his family admitted to his mother and father, "I didn't realize how exhausting your job is; and I can tell you that being a dying person is also exhausting."

A council circle can take place in a hospital room, a home, or a meadow in the high mountains. We might bring a candle, a flower, or a bowl of water to help us make the border crossing from the busyness and complexity of our lives to the intimacy and truth we want to call forth. Placing something in the center gives the council focus. Another important element in council practice is the "talking piece." The talking piece can be anything: a seashell, a family heirloom, a Bible, a ceremonial object, or something found in the place where council is held. I often use a stone that I found years ago during a pilgrimage to Mount Kailash, the sacred mountain of Tibet. This piece has now been held in the hands of thousands of people. Whoever holds the talking piece holds our undivided attention. The talking piece can have a magnetic and protective quality, allowing a speaker to focus, as if on an object of meditation.

Silence is another treasure we bring to council, and beginning council with a moment of silence gives us the opportunity to drop down into our hearts. Dying people in particular are often in a purgatory of routinized communication, and they crave silence. I remember sitting with a friend who only wanted silence in his hospital room. Idle chatter, redundant questions, fake solace were not what he needed. So we two sat in council with each other sharing silence, handing back and forth a small stone. This was grace for both of us.

To come together in council, we sit together roughly in a circle, whether there are two of us or twenty. Before beginning, someone reminds us all aloud of the council's guiding principles:

- Speaking from the heart
- Listening from the heart
- Speaking concisely
- Speaking spontaneously

These four crucial skills can keep us steady in the midst of profound complexity.

First, in council we speak from the heart. Some of us are used to speaking from the head, speaking in terms of philosophical, social, psychological, and political ideas. But council is about transparency, authenticity, and intimate revelation. We are called to speak from personal experience, opening this treasure box through stories and through expressing our feelings in direct and unburdening ways.

We can also let silence speak for us, inviting all into a greater sense of interiority. In council, no one has to speak if he does not wish to. He can simply hold the talking piece and then pass it on.

Next comes listening from the heart. Deep listening means listening in tolerance and inclusiveness—what the Quakers call "devout listening." Council removes the option of interrupting a speaker, so that each individual can speak without being afraid of being cut off. Also, we who hear have a chance to relax into spacious listening without judgment or prejudice, listening not only to what is said but also to what is left unsaid. As we listen, many responses may arise: memories, associations, insights, criticism, agreement. We can be aware that these narratives are happening within us, and be able to let them go.

As listeners, we don't respond or share our associations until it is our time to speak. This can be difficult when the subjects are tough ones. People may bring their deepest suffering forward, or break down in tears. The impulse for most of us is to intervene, to give support and to take away the suffering of the person as quickly as possible, because it is unbearable for us. But the most skillful response is not to intervene but simply to bear witness. This is a profound way for us to share suffering in a situation of trust and support. It might be a struggle to hear the perspectives of others. But that's what we're asked to do—to listen to the wisdom of the circle.

As we begin to listen with a new quality of inclusiveness and patience, the practice helps us shift from reactive to attentive listening. Each speaker is like a new world opening up, and the listeners experience a collective understanding that transcends language. In learning deep listening, I invite hearers to consider that this is the speaker's last day on earth and to give this one the quality of attention we would give to someone who will die tomorrow. Can we receive unconditionally whatever she is saying? Respectful and open listening elicits deeper truth from us as we speak about our concerns, fears, and feelings of shame and rejection.

Then, too, we value concision; we want to go to the heart of the matter. We want to recognize that every moment is precious. When it is our turn to speak, we need to pause for a moment and come into the truth of the heart at that moment. We speak to the truth of the situation as genuinely as we can. Council calls for us to develop clear speaking so that we are really in the marrow of our being, as well as an economy of speech so that all those who wish to share their insights or confusion have time to do so. Many of us find the discipline of being concise difficult. We have to rely on the collective to hold the whole story. If we surrender to the group, rest assured someone will touch upon that piece we could not address.

Finally, we speak spontaneously and in an unpremeditated way. In doing council over the years, sometimes I find myself rehearsing internally what I will say. At such moments I ask myself, What is really happening at this very moment? Am I able to bring forward my experience? Is this the right time to share what I see? Am I able to trust, and go deeper than what I think I know?

Once a young Native American man was tried for a crime. When it was time for him to testify, he was asked to swear to tell the truth, the whole truth, and nothing but the truth. Trembling, he looked at the judge and said in a barely audible voice, "I can't." The judge insisted that this was standard court procedure. The young man began to weep as he replied, "But sir, who can know the whole truth?" Only a community can hold the truth, if we trust the alchemy of its process, journeying though we do not know the destination. Council asks, Can we bear to look at what we have not told ourselves? Can we hear what we do not know? No one answer can hold the truth of a good heart, but the experience itself of council's community can help heal us. The wisdom of the circle will always prevail, and deep sharing and listening can bring us home.

# 12

## Wounded Healers
### *The Shadow Side of Caregiving*

Y OU PROBABLY are already familiar with the archetypes of caregiving, negative as well as positive. On the one hand there's the selfless saint, possessing seemingly endless resources of compassion
and generosity. On the other there's the martyr—bitter, exhausted, and
unable to perform the smallest service without simmering resentment.
While caregiving can be one of the most noble and useful practices life
has for us, one that is healing for both dying people and their support-
ers, a glowing, beatified image of service can cast a very long, very dark
shadow. Strangely, the more glorified our idealization of the caregiver
who's never tired or irritable or needy, the more likely we are to invite that
other archetype instead, as aspects of the shadow emerge and make their
way forward.

Sandy's caregivers, for example, found themselves falling prey to their
fatigue toward the end of her illness. Every few months, the dying woman
moved to the edge of death, then back toward life again. These rough tides
began to take their toll on Sandy's friends, who had been providing a home
for her as well as taking care of her for years. Worn out and disheartened,
her friends became suspicious that she was clinging to life, unable to surrender to the inevitable.

Finally—when Sandy became extremely demanding, angry, and chaotic—her friends had no more personal resources with which to help her. In attempting to care completely for Sandy, they had taken on more than they had bargained for. They had not created a plan for the long haul—and long is exactly what it was. At that point, they tried to find someplace else for her to stay.

Sandy fortunately did not have to move; a new group of friends stepped in to help, visiting every day, sitting with her for hours and sharing practice with her. She was particularly interested in the Tibetan practice of consciousness transference at the time of death. She also wanted to be held and read to. This new group of caregivers enabled her old friends to pull away from Sandy to a healthier distance and to relax somewhat. Yet they still felt ashamed, as if they had somehow failed her.

As time passed, Sandy's pain became so extreme that she was given large amounts of medication so she could rest. People sat with her twenty-four hours a day as she moved closer to death. And then one day she was gone. Bearing witness to her death was challenging, but it was even harder to be with the pain of friends who had withdrawn after their energy had been used up. All the love and support that the rest of us offered could not allay their guilty belief that they should have done more. Yet perhaps what they really could have done was *less*.

This situation has continued to serve me as a hard-learned reminder of the power of the shadow. Being familiar with its intimate aspects, the various kinds of mishaps and miseries that can draw a caregiver into deep and cold water, makes it possible to correct our course, and encourages us to get more help before we're in over our heads.

Once a student asked me, "What is the shadow of the bodhisattva?" I responded, "Helping other beings." That sounds strange until you consider that bodhisattvas have realized nonduality, responding to the suffering of the world like that wooden puppet whose strings are being pulled by the whole of creation. There is no "I" doing a good deed for "another," but simply choiceless responsiveness, combined with the feeling that the self is not local but existing in oneness with everything. The right hand, we say in Zen, is just taking care of the left hand. No big deal. If there's a big deal—if there's a you helping other beings, rescuing other beings, then the shadow of the bodhisattva can cause real trouble.

Following are some of the common difficulties that caregivers have encountered, some of the roles we may find ourselves enacting. Don't feel bad if you find yourself here. The only reason I am able to enumerate these problems is that every single one of them has been part of my own experience in working with the dying, and most of my colleagues and friends can say the same. There's a saying in Japan about the wobbly, round-bottomed Bodhidharma doll that children play with: *Fall down eight times, get up nine.* Ultimately, there is no one right way to be with dying. We do the very best that we can, and humility becomes our companion along the way as we fall down and get up again. And sometimes we learn the most from our most painful experiences.

## The Hero

Heroism can drive a caregiver far beyond what is sensible and compassionate. You often hear someone caught in the role of the Hero insisting, "I'm the only one who can help . . . there's no one else to do it but me." Are your caretaking hours long by most people's standards? Are you recommending extreme medical interventions, even against the dying one's wishes? If you find yourself feeling alone and confronting challenges on all sides without any support, you've probably fallen into the heroic role. Another word for the hero is *rescuer.*

Perhaps an unconscious desire for gratitude and reassurance fuels heroism; too often, those who serve the dying are doing so to fulfill unmet emotional needs. Heroes also crave acknowledgment from the community. Their identity is forged on the anvil of good acts. While we might imagine how nice it would be to hear the dying person or his family say, "I couldn't do this without you," letting this hunger for acknowledgment drive caregiving can lead us into being overextended, and not being fully present for the dying person (who might have little interest in his caregiver's needs). Can you let the practice of caregiving itself be your fulfillment? Finding other, more appropriate ways to get emotional needs met—through other people or activities—will help.

The best antidote to the Hero is to share the responsibility. Work to involve others in caregiving. Many Heroes become so attached to their importance or the specialness of their relationship to the dying person that they make it almost impossible for anyone else to help. Another driver of the Hero is fear. If you're stuck in the Hero, start by giving up some control. Trust other caregivers, and allow their participation. Developing clear boundaries serves those with whom we work as well as ourselves. A helpful phrase might be, "May I accept my own limits with compassion." It may seem incredibly difficult at first, but the benefits are many—including the rare opportunity to explore our own issues of attachment.

## The Martyr

In many ways, the Martyr is just a late-stage, burned-out Hero. For a family member who is the primary caregiver, a physician on call, a nurse working the night shift or overtime, or a friend sitting long hours with the dying person because there is no family member to help, the overwhelming physical and emotional demands of caregiving can eventually push you from fatigue into resentment. The martyr often suffers from compassion fatigue and secondary trauma, having been overexposed to suffering and unable to cope with more exposure.

You'll know the Martyr is present when you hear yourself saying yes to everything (what I call "knee-jerk compassion") but inwardly hating it all. Or perhaps helping when help isn't needed? The Martyr proclaims exhaustion and never has enough time to do what is needed to be done. Before responding automatically to requests, it might be a good idea to examine your motivations (as with the Hero). What would best serve both the dying person and you?

Exhausted Martyrs such as Sandy's friends finally grow impatient with the dying process. They may secretly wish that this person would "let go and die," saying to each other in private, "She just can't surrender," or "He won't let go." To guard against being taken over by the Martyr, take the powerful medicine of good self-care. Build resilience for attending to the needs of others by attending to your own needs. Pace yourself. Make breathing room in your life with nourishing activity. Create a schedule that gives you days off. Rest and take care of yourself to restore your perspective (it's possible to find moments of profound rest even in the midst of crowded, busy circumstances). And if your acceptance has run its course, find someone fresh who can sit with the person who is dying. There is no shame in stepping out of the field of practice when you are exhausted, and it's better than grimly hanging in there and becoming abusive, which I have seen happen more than once.

## THE PARENT

Even if you actually are the dying person's parent, identifying with the role isn't necessarily the best way to relate to her, or to yourself. When we become the intrusive Parent, we start to exhibit behaviors that are controlling and literally patronizing. You'll know the Parent is present if you hear yourself using the imperative voice, as we do with small children ("Don't do that!" "Take your pills," etc.), or making statements like, "You don't know what's best for you." Perhaps an even more accurate name for the Parent would be the Cruise Director. If you catch yourself micromanaging, giving orders, or telling everyone what should be happening, pause. Turn to the dying one and the family, and ask them what they want and need. Practicing even a little not-knowing allows the truth of each situation to emerge without our having to direct or control it.

Treating a dying person as if he's incompetent is another form of being parental, and it usually arises from our insecurity and distrust. As the dying person passes through the stages of death, he will gradually lose control anyway, without our taking it away prematurely. One of the great gifts we can offer is control over whatever he still wants to manage. Let him do as he wants for as long as he can, whether it be walking to the toilet or deciding what to eat and with whom to visit. Don't take over this person's life just as he is losing it; trust his inherent wisdom, and practice letting go.

If I had to sum up conscious, responsible caregiving in a phrase, I might say, "Let the dying one take the lead." Too often we treat dying people as if they were already dead, with no voice of their own, no opportunity to choose how they will die. Letting the dying one take the lead really requires us to be with not-knowing and to bear witness to things as they are. It requires courage and confidence in each being's natural, inherent wisdom as her life is being wound into the immediate experience of death.

Sita was a young Indian woman dying of breast cancer. My coworker Katherine volunteered to support Sita and her family, and in the process she learned an immense amount about their cultural differences. Many of Sita's family's gender issues, religious beliefs, and customs around dying were completely new to her. Katherine's sensitivity and her willingness to experience not-knowing helped her discover the best way to be with Sita and her often emotionally volatile family.

After several weeks, Sita's hospice nurses said that she displayed the physical signs of impending death and would probably die within three to five days. Sita's family began their ritual funeral preparations, with her male relatives shaving their heads and fasting. Others painted traditional colors on Sita's forehead and along her hairline as she lay in a deep coma. They arranged for a restaurant to serve traditional foods for the breaking-fast gathering that would happen the morning after she died.

On the day Sita was expected to die, Katherine came to the house to support the family. But instead of a deathbed scene, Katherine found Sita sitting up in bed playing cards! Sita put down her cards when she saw Katherine, and asked her insistently, very distraught, "Did you really think I was dying?" Katherine realized that the young woman was deeply troubled because everyone had been so quick to mobilize for her death. She feared her family wanted her to hurry up and die—after all, they had been in this crisis with her for five years.

When we practice having the mind of not-knowing, then we're most able to help intuitively, even when we don't quite know the right thing to do. Katherine didn't go to the library and read books on Hindu religious and cultural practice; she kept her heart open and her intention focused on not-knowing, and these led her into right action. Because she abided in not-knowing, accepting that Sita would have her own way of doing things—even dying on her own timetable—Katherine was able to reassure Sita, and return her sense of control over her own death. Even if we think we clearly read the signs of active dying, death's timing is unpredictable, and we must let the dying one take the lead.

A caregiver who's been taken over by the Parent may interfere with someone's dying in a very direct way: talking too much, giving unwanted advice, trying to divert or entertain the dying one, probing for information or asking emotionally loaded questions when the dying person would prefer privacy, or sharing personal problems in a misguided bid to establish intimacy. All these violate emotional boundaries; we violate physical boundaries when we refuse to leave the dying person alone, or insist on physical contact at a time when what is needed is simplicity, not entanglement. Not all physical contact is inappropriate; holding and touching can be very soothing and reassuring for the dying. But try to be aware of your motivation when giving physical support, and make sure you know whether it is wanted. Dying people are usually in the process of letting go of relationships, not initiating them or complicating existing ones.

Also be aware that people who are dying may not want much company, preferring to rest or be alone with their thoughts; and they certainly don't feel like entertaining. Do not overstay your welcome just because you can't tell when it is time to leave, you're afraid "something might happen," or you think you are needed absolutely every minute. Ask the dying person if she would like some quiet time.

The best cure for the Parent is, as gently as possible, to look very clearly at what you are doing. With honesty, examine what's motivating you and what effects your behavior is having on others. Let your kindness and unconditional love guide you to be present rather than paternalistic.

## THE EXPERT

The Expert often appears in overextended medical professionals, or in caregivers who aren't comfortable with the strong feelings stirred up in them by being with dying. Someone seized by the Expert is trying to cope by acting in a clinical or "professional" manner, distancing themselves from the uncertainty of the situation and hiding behind the role, treating the dying person as an inanimate object, neglecting her or talking in front of her as if she weren't there. (Even if someone is unconscious, your presence, speech, and even your thoughts can have an impact on her dying.) Do you avoid making eye contact, avoid connecting in a genuine way?

Do you release tension by discussing her and her family in a way that violates confidentiality?

When the Expert has us avoiding our feelings, the solution is actually to face them directly. Talk to someone you trust, with whom it's safe to admit your fear, anger, or sadness. It's completely natural for these emotions to be brought up in the presence of illness, pain, and loss, and it's especially common for old, unacknowledged grief to be activated. Staying open to the discomfort of these feelings gives us a precious chance to bear witness. Don't turn away from the grief, but work with it as you go along, using it as a way to deepen your compassion and a chance to examine your expectations and your long-held beliefs. Thank the Expert for trying to protect you, and then let your distancing melt into intimacy. Embracing this experience—*this* one, with all its suffering—can be a catalyst to awaken your good heart.

## THE PRIEST

It's possible for caregivers to become spiritually inflated, getting an emotional high from being around suffering (strange as that may sound). As with the Expert, that inflation can keep us from being with our own discomfort. We're acting in the role of the Priest when we think we alone have all the answers, and know what is spiritually right for the dying one. If you hear yourself giving a lot of lofty-sounding advice or "preaching," the Priest has probably arrived.

One of the Priest's most insidious tendencies is to believe that we can define a "good death" for the person for whom we're caring. We then fall into the trap of being subtly coercive, manipulating the dying person and his family to conform with the prevailing notion of the "best" way to die. The Priest thinks that doing things a certain way will guarantee a good death, insisting on a particular spiritual practice or persuading the person to die at home when he really wants hospital support (or taking him to the hospital when he would rather be home). Sometimes there's the belief that the whole family needs to be involved, when actually the dying one feels complete without a lot of people around him and wants to die peacefully.

The antidote for this role is simply not-knowing. Whenever you feel convinced that you know what is right, stop for a minute and consider. Each death is unique, and mysteriously perfect just as it is. Of course, we want the best for each dying person, but having expectations of how someone should die doesn't help anyone. When you feel like putting pressure on the dying one to die in a particular way, consciously relax and let go of your expectations. Give up this notion of a good death—or that you have any idea what it will look like.

Dying is a full-time job. Expect dying people to be preoccupied with learning everything they can about their condition and coping with the radical changes they are experiencing. Expect them to be absorbed in their pain and illness, their spiritual practice, and saying goodbye to loved ones. Most are passing through an overwhelming experience, and in addition, it demands a huge amount of energy to attend to all the people who are suddenly in contact with them—health care professionals, social workers, insurance agents, lawyers, hospice workers, friends, and family—and to sort through complicated information, trying to figure out all the questions: *What are these medications? What are these procedures going to do to me? How much longer will I be here?*

Dying can be like an intense climate with wild weather and extremes of heat and cold. We will probably be wounded by and wound others in its process. Because we're in unknown territory, dying gives rise to completely unexpected, unpredictable situations that put us on the spot and test our commitment. Our roles too often protect us from weathering our own maturation, and from offering our best to those who suffer.

When the shadow of caretaking shows its ugliest face and we feel the most lost and confused, it's then that we stand on the very ground for opening our hearts and letting go of our concepts. Can we be truly compassionate with ourselves when we fail to be flawless caregivers, and with the dying person when she fails to die in the way we think she should? Buried in the coals of this fire lie the deepest opportunities to practice not-knowing and bearing witness—and, finally, to trust in presence. Perhaps afterward, we'll find ourselves more available, somewhat more humble, and wiser for it all.

## MEDITATION

### *Four Profound Reminders*

Let your body settle and gently bring your attention to your breath. Relax and let yourself be aware of the flow of thoughts, feelings, and sensations without getting involved with them. When you find yourself clinging to thoughts, return to the breath, without feeling pressure.

1. Having settled into your body, please remember how precious this human life is. During this life you have encountered so much that has been helpful, including good teachers, the possibility of having a spiritual life, and teachings that inspire and guide you. Many people have helped you, and you have had the joy of helping others. Although you have suffered, you have also had many moments in your life that have been good. Please appreciate the preciousness of your life, what you might be able to realize through it, and how you may be able to help others as well.

2. Now contemplate the truth of impermanence. Look at your mind. Every thought and feeling that you have ever had has changed in one way or another. Your body, too, is constantly changing. One day it will die. Buddha, Christ, Muhammad—all the great teachers of the past have died. Everything in the phenomenal world will change, and one day, sooner or later, will cease to exist. Impermanence is real. Death is inevitable.

3. Now contemplate the truth of cause and effect. You yourself are a result of an endless chain of causes and effects involving your parents and ancestors stretching back through time. Before your human ancestors, there were animal and plant ancestors. And before the ancestors of mammal and blue-green algae, there were the elements. This chain of cause and effect is endless. Your relations are endless, and your past actions are like a shadow that follows you everywhere. Your future is also being laid down at this very moment. Consider that kindness and compassion give rise to good effects, and aggression and greed give rise to suffering. Do what you can to decrease suffering for yourself and others. Realize that you can purify your life by doing good for others and by atoning

for the suffering you have caused yourself and others. You can transform this suffering into wisdom. Realize the truth of consequences.

4. Finally, consider the truth of suffering—birth, old age, sickness, death, getting what you do not want, not getting what you do want, and losing that which you cherish. So often you have felt that this or that will make you happy, will finally bring you peace. You might have worked very hard for these things—a good relationship, a nice house, a satisfying job. Yet sooner or later you will lose all these things. They themselves can also cause you to suffer. Consider the truth of ill-being, and the great benefit of being free of suffering. Contemplate what it would be to live a life without fear. Know that deathless enlightenment is here at this very moment. Can you relax your grip on what you think is real and open your life to whatever arises? Can you see through the illusion of past, present, and future? Can you let go of the reference points of solidity, identity, and separateness? Can you relax and open to things as they are? Can you plunge into life at this very moment and accept and learn from all of it? Let confidence arise in the truth of the present moment. Be there for it.

Relax as you experience this focused awareness, sense of inquiry, and presence, and remember who you really are, and why you are here.

# PART THREE

## Making a Whole Cloth

FOR THE ONE who is dying, the third and final phase in this rite of change is the experience of encountering death. Those of us who remain behind return to the ordinary world for now, to continue the work of not-knowing, bearing witness, and compassionate action.

The third tenet, compassionate action, asks us to make a whole cloth of all the pieces of our lives, to include everything that has happened and to reject nothing. What does this mean? Like the Buddhist priests who sew their robes from discarded scraps of cloth, the dying one and those who care and then grieve for her make a whole cloth from all the tattered fragments of their experience of the journey.

On the path of the caregiver, we experience healing by doing what needs to be done, for ourselves as well as for others. For the dying person, healing means letting go into the unknown, being with the rich inevitability of elemental dissolution, and knowing the singular taste of freedom from all cares and burdens, including those of body and mind.

For those who grieve, we heal when we mature through our loss, learning to accept loss and change. This brokenheartedness that we call sorrow—our kinship with the now-invisible other—is really a lotus flower nourished by the cold and murky waters of grief. Grief can bloom into humility, faith, and tenderness when we hold it with patience and respect, and find a sane relationship to our sadness without being overwhelmed.

This is the third phase in living and dying, being one with the complete truth of caring, surrender, and grieving—all expressions of oneness with the great and subtle truth of what is.

# 13

## Doorways to Truth
### *From Fear to Liberation*

WHAT I HAVE learned from each of the dying people with whom I have worked is that the road to death is always matchless. Just as we live in our own way, so each of us dies in our own way. Our difficulties in approaching death, however, usually have a common root, the root of fear—fear of change, fear of losing our separate self and all that we seem to possess, and fear of the uncharted territory we're entering. Following are six common responses to dying and death. Exploring them, we can see that there's no "wrong" way to die, and that it's possible to find liberation even in the most difficult situations.

### FEARING DEATH
Many of us will naturally feel afraid when we first face the truth of death or a catastrophic diagnosis. We fear pain and its management; we fear the loss of all that is precious to us, including our capacities, our possessions, our relationships, our dignity, and our life; and we fear the unknown—the annihilation of the self. Fear often lies behind attempts to sustain life through heroic medical interventions, regardless of the resulting quality of life.

Accepting death as a natural part of life sounds simple—all that stands in our way is fear of dying well—and of living well. Although fear can be a terrible obstacle as death approaches, it can also be an ally, as it can push dying people and their families to reach out for help of a spiritual nature when medicine might have little to offer. Fear can help us see what is truly important, and compel us to prioritize. Within our fear, we may discover, are precious seeds of wisdom. Because of this, I am very careful not to make judgments about a person's attitude toward dying—be it fear, denial, sorrow, defiance, acceptance, or liberation.

Many of us have experienced fear in the core of our being. We can work with fear through practice as we offer space to our own fears and those of others. By bearing witness in this way we can help a dying person and her community open to the good work of attending fear and letting it draw us through its tight fist into the open hand and heart of acceptance and no fear. Mustering the courage to be present for our old acquaintance fear can open the great door to truly living one's dying. In this way, even a fearful response to dying can be liberating.

## DENYING DEATH

Although we often consider denial to be an unhealthy response to difficulties, denial can also be a positive adaptation to a catastrophic situation. In addition, it may well have a wisdom of its own.

When Mary, who had lymphoma, came to see me, I was moved by her appearance. Because of chemotherapy, she had no hair, no eyebrows, no eyelashes. Flaring from her neck were huge tumors that made her look like a beautiful reptile.

Although her friends had told me Mary was in denial, I found her denial curiously radiant. In our first interview, she leaned toward me and said, "I am not going to die." At that instant, I felt she spoke the truth. When we cut through the illusion of ourselves as solid and separate entities, we may well come to the conclusion that nobody dies.

One day Mary's network of friends, about twenty-five women in all, came together. We sat in council and I asked the simple question: "What are you feeling?" They responded with suffering and frustration. I could not blame this circle of good-hearted women. Something was definitely not working for them. For one thing it bothered them all that Mary was "in denial." On another note they had not quite got themselves organized, they felt demoralized, and their care of their friend was erratic. They seemed to be in a world apart from her, and at the same time they loved her and wanted to do their best for her as she was dying.

We explored the question of denial and how Mary's refusal to accept the imminence of her death could on some level be a reflection of her insight into deathlessness. This was a possibility that might free them to accept Mary's attitude of denial.

We also listened deeply to one another. Mary's friends could not ignore their shared fears and frustrations, once they were spoken aloud. When they heard one another, they shifted to a position of compassion for themselves, as well as a greater understanding of their friend's perspective on dying. We then set out to do the most practical thing, which was to make a schedule.

Over the ensuing weeks, it seemed as though everything went much more smoothly. People showed up at Mary's on time and worked with accepting her just as she was. I also was part of the schedule, and had the joy of sitting with her several times a week. She and I listened to music, sat in silence, and occasionally talked about simple spiritual issues. And Mary stayed in "denial" up until the moment of her death, when she died peacefully. Her last words were "I am not dying."

It's easy to consider denial as some kind of pathology. However, in being with dying, we simply do not know when it might be serving a positive or healing function. "The difficulty," said philosopher Ludwig Wittgenstein, "is to realize the groundlessness of our believing."* This is truly notknowing. Deep down inside we are all aware that we are going to die. If we activate the spirit of hope or wisdom through denial, as Mary did, that is our own business. In some situations it can be of great help and bring peace into our lives. In Mary's case, perhaps what we were calling "denial" was her knowledge that some part of her would never die. I did not know then, and now years later, I still cannot draw a conclusion, except that her moment of death was marked by great peace.

---

* Ludwig Wittgenstein, *On Certainty,* §166, trans. Denis Paul and G. E. M. Anscombe (Oxford, U.K.: Blackwell Publishing, 1996), 469.

## GRIEVING DEATH

The response to a catastrophic diagnosis can open a great wound of sadness, the real grief over the anticipated loss of a life not yet fully lived. Earlier I wrote about Ann, diagnosed with an aggressive glioblastoma. In her early forties, she was a creative researcher and physician. At the time of her diagnosis, she was in the midst of a research project on the very tumor that was now afflicting her—a strange irony. Often she was brave, sometimes objective, and at times unbearably sad.

What gifts could this great sadness give her, I quietly asked myself. This was a sorrow that was unbearable for those around her. Who could give comfort to someone so totally brokenhearted? Really no one could, though all tried.

Sometimes Ann would call me, and I listened to her grief pouring from the phone. Like dark water issuing from a deep chasm inside of her, her cries were like those of a mother whose child had just died, of a wife whose husband had just been killed in war. The wave of unbearable sadness was always followed by a wave of relief, however, a wave that washed the shoreline clean of debris. Not discouraging or consoling her, just being there for her in the midst of her sorrow became a means for me to help her clear the way for a greater acceptance of the inevitability of her death and the loss of all that was precious to her, including her husband, her friends, her work, and finally her life.

Although at times I found it hard to bear witness to Ann's grief, I also saw its value in helping her to scour out her heart so that it became bigger as active dying approached. To have robbed her of the opportunity of expressing that sadness by overconsoling her or trying to distract her would have taken away a piece of her life that had gone unexpressed by her years of optimism. Ann's natural sadness gave her the chance to open to a deep level of compassion—and it became her guide into death.

## DEFYING DEATH

When death is viewed as an enemy, then the urge to fight can grow strong and emphatic. Defying death, a friend of mine fought his end at every turn. He did everything possible to prolong his life, including exotic medical treatments, unusual alternative treatments, Tibetan practices, visualizations, prayer, writing, and working until almost the day of his death. To many of us his battle was both inspiring and terrifying.

Buddhist teachings say that the odds of being born as a human are as low as the odds of a blind sea turtle who surfaces just once every hundred thousand years, rising into the embrace of a floating golden yoke. It is during our precious human lives that we can help others transform their suffering and realize our own enlightenment. So, although Buddhists accept death as inevitable, most Buddhists, like everyone else, will do whatever they can to prolong their lives.

This friend was no exception. He defied death until death took him, and in the years that he lived beyond his prognosis, I can say that he helped many, many of us.

## ACCEPTING DEATH

My first teacher was a Huichol healer from Mexico, Don José Ríos, whom we called Matsúwa. When he was very old, one morning Matsúwa walked out from his hut on his mountaintop in order to die alone in the wilderness. He accepted his death, like everything else he had accepted in his life. But Matsúwa's family was not ready to let him go. After a few days, they realized what he had done and went in search of him. Under a tree, far from the village, he lay there—peaceful, weak, starving, and ready to give it all up. He was carried back to the village and persuaded back to life. I think Matsúwa was pretty disappointed in having his plan interrupted. He had accepted his death, and his family had not.

This story is not so uncommon. I can't tell you how many people I've encountered who have been resuscitated, only to be angry or disappointed that they had not been allowed to accept death on their own terms. To die an accepting death requires deep presence of mind and a radical ability to embrace whatever each moment brings, including being saved from death.

## LIBERATING DEATH

Perhaps the most fortunate and rarest response to death is that of liberated realization. Various spiritual traditions look on death as a precious and powerful opportunity for enlightenment. Whether or not enlightenment is possible at the moment of death, the practices that prepare one for this possibility also bring one closer to the bone of life.

Coming to terms with the truth of impermanence is one of the most important ways for us to transform our relationship to dying and death. If we are able to realize that everything we cherish will be lost, we will not be so fearful of death. We can understand that it is simply the natural order. Realizing impermanence is itself a profound purification of our passion and aggression and can inspire us to help others. As the Zen Buddhist service says, "Now you have realized the world of impermanence; this is rare and inconceivable."

Not only great teachers die enlightened deaths. Gisela had been through two rounds of melanoma, and the doctors finally told her there was nothing more to be done. At seventy-five, she had been a committed student of meditation for many years and was a genuinely altruistic person; though her illness sometimes made her sad, she also seemed to have a strong attitude of realism and acceptance. When she heard that her bone marrow had been overwhelmed with the cancer, Gisela said quietly and lightly, "Bummer." Afterward, in talking with me, she shared, "This is not as hard as I thought it would be."

Every encounter in the short six days between her terminal diagnosis and her death was marked by peace and joy. From time to time, she lifted out of the deep waters of dying to express joy to those by her side. For those of us who sat vigil through her last days, we could clearly see her riding toward death with natural courage and deep ease. Her body unbound itself smoothly, and the moment of her death was radiant; rainbows appeared in the sky over her house as she died. After her death, we sat with her for three more days. Her body remained unusually fresh and beautiful, a smile gracing her lips. We all felt something extraordinary had transpired in her death; her liberation was palpable.

One who is free of fear knows that at the deepest level of realization there is no suffering, no birth, no death. Each moment is new and complete—right now being born, right now dying. All phenomena are in flux. Riding the waves of impermanence, the elements come together as form and dissolve into formlessness. In some sense we are never born; we will never die.

The Tibetan yogi Milarepa was afraid of death because he had once lived a harmful life, and had killed other people. He understood that dying can bring up everything we fear, and he feared that the harm he had caused others would besiege his life and determine his rebirth. He longed to realize his true nature before it was too late. In the end, after much practice, he was able to say that the fear of death had led him to the snowcapped mountains where he meditated on the uncertainty of the moment of his death. In this way, he reached the eternal refuge of the true nature of mind, and his fear vanished into the distance.

At that point, Milarepa experienced a real triumph over terror. When we realize our true nature—that absolute space free of birth and death—it is possible to dwell in this relative body without fear of loss. We can leave behind fearfulness, denial, sorrow, defiance, and even acceptance, to reach toward true liberation. This is our practice for a realized death.

## MEDITATION

### Walking Meditation

One day, I walked with my father down the corridor of the hospital where he was dying. The respiratory therapist realized that my father and I were very comfortable with each other and that I might enjoy encouraging him to move his old bones and get his breath going. I wrapped my right arm around him, and began to walk slowly, in synchrony with his breath. Step by careful step, we made our way down the hallway, breathing and stepping with the pace of his breath. This is something I do every day at home in the zendo, but without my arms around my fragile, beautiful father.

Walking meditation is a practice where we bring the mind, breath, and body together. We can fold our hands together at the waist, and let the body settle in the same way we do in sitting meditation. The shoulders are soft, the face relaxed, the spine straight and alive, and the breath deep in the body. And then we take a step. We begin by inhaling and gently stepping with our left foot. When the foot touches the ground, we might be on our exhale. We just let our attention sink with the breath into the foot, and feel solid and present as we complete our exhalation. In the gap before the next inhalation, we might pause and allow a feeling of letting go.

On the next inhalation, we step with the right foot. Sometimes, we might want to really settle our mind, and then we can pay close attention to the sensation of our heel touching the floor, then the ball of our foot, and then our toes. We can feel each toe as it touches the floor, and then we might pause until the breath is complete and feel the strength of just being present.

This is the practice of one breath, one step. We can go even slower, as is taught in Burma, when we slowly and carefully lift the foot with an inhalation and exhalation. And then gently place the ball of the foot and toes on the floor with an inhalation and exhalation. Or we can walk faster, with one whole step on the inhalation, and one whole step on the exhalation. No matter what our velocity, the structure of the walking is normal—that is to say, we don't lift the foot high off the ground or hold the foot in the air in midstep. If we are doing a very slow walking meditation, we just lift the heel off the floor but keep the ball of the foot rooted until we have completed our breath cycle.

If you are walking outdoors or down a hospital corridor and you want to practice walking meditation, just relax, breathe normally, and try taking two steps on the inhale and three steps on the exhale. Find the number of steps to a breath that works for you.

Vietnamese teacher Thich Nhat Hanh encourages his students to use verses with walking practice. When I am outdoors, I might say, "Walking (one step) the green (one step) earth (one step)." Or if I am walking down a corridor, I might simply count my steps, or say to myself, "One breath, one step." Sometimes I make up a verse appropriate for a particular moment. For example, when walking with my father, I said to myself, "I am grateful (one step) for my father (one step)."

A young student of mine from Nepal had never practiced walking meditation before, though he had lived in a monastery since he was six years old. It really surprised him that the practice was so refreshing. I sometimes encourage doctors and nurses to use this as a way to help them transform the often rushed or harried way they move through the hospital. I've also found the practice to be a wonderful gift to give an old person, or someone who is sick and needs to move. Walking along with the elderly and frail brings you together in a new and intimate way that can engender deep trust.

# 14

## Embracing the Road
### *How We Remember, Assess, Express, and Find Meaning*

A s MY FRIEND Steven entered the early phase of active dying, he wrote me expressing his concern and frustration with the tubes delivering oxygen up his nose. My response to him:

Dear Steven,

You are compromised and this is a hard road you have been traveling. You have helped so many, been there for so many, and now you face death with the very atmosphere squeezed out of your lungs. As you have taught me to accept the truth of each moment, no matter how raw, so such moments are being offered to you, and you cannot refuse.

In Buddhism, we think about, meditate on, and look forward to death. And when it approaches us, our mettle is tested.

I pray you have no expectations, but also know that whatever you go through, they say that the moment of release is the great gate to freedom. I hope they are telling the truth. I believe it, and yet the proof is in our experience of it.

*Love, Joan*

Dear Joan,

I welcome death. It's the dying that's the pisser. How can we make it easier?

Thank you for the feast you brought to my table.

*Steven*


Dear Steven,

The Supreme Meal is made of all of the ingredients of this life, even the sour and bitter ones.

You asked me how can we make dying easier? I must tell you the truth: I don't know. But here is some simple counsel.

Find peace in small things.

Appreciate your life, all the good you have done. This is really important.

Consider how others are suffering, maybe in a similar way to you. Compassion is a treasure box.

Make peace with those around you.

But the truth is, we just do the best we can. Somehow we burn through it all sooner or later.

I feel the horizon of dying may seem really small when we are going through it, but it wraps around the Milky Way and takes us home to the boundlessness that we really are.

Oh, dear Steven, I find it difficult to accept that you are dying so hard. I wish it otherwise for you.

And this is the way it is: raw and not predictable.

You are in my prayers, my heart,

*Joan*


Dear Joan,

I will return to you, to ask more questions, before I join the Milky Way, if/when the fates of karma allow.

I feel your compassion so deeply in my heart, and I cannot ignore your wisdom.

I'm not sure what you mean by "dying so hard." Should I die like a worm or should I die like a cougar? Either way is fine. Are you telling me I should "go gentle into that good night"?

Why are these ashes spilled? What about my woman, my family, my children and grandchildren? You were always such a teacher about karma.

You too are in my prayers and in my heart.

*Steven*

There was no more energy on his part to write. Slowly his lungs filled up and that was that. His hospice doctor and his wife breathed with him as he met his death. I was told he died like a cougar.

Steven wanted to know the meaning of his living and dying, and as he neared death, he looked through the stuff of his life to see what lay there, and he sought meaning in his relationships and in the poetry and songs he loved. Though I do not know for certain if he found an answer that satisfied him, I do know that this quest for meaning is not at all unusual. There's quite often a desire on the part of the dying person to remember, review, assess, and find meaning in his life. If the dying person is able, completing these tasks can bring about an astonishing amount of healing for the one who dies as well as for his survivors.

A grandchild sits by a bedside listening to an old man tell his life story; a tape recorder captures his words, preserves his history, and gives dignity and importance to the telling. A family helps a mother dying of breast cancer make a scrapbook reflecting her life; her bed is filled with photos, friends, and children as this process happens. A small altar is put together by a dying man and his family and friends; the altar is adorned with treasures of a life well lived. A good man with Alzheimer's shares his heart and truth with his wife as his mind slowly but surely falls into twilight; when the last glimmers of his conceptual mind fade into darkness, she reaches through the void to assure him his words and wisdom will live on through her writing. A dying patient requests that a video camera sit in her room, and she talks to it, telling us how it is to die and how it has been to live; years after her death, her sister sets up a telephone hotline for people with catastrophic illnesses, knowing how important it is to the dying to be listened to—and how important it is for the rest of us to hear.

Zen hospice founder Frank Ostaseski tells a wonderful story about a hip young man with green hair and studs in his ears who went to volunteer at a hospice in the San Francisco Bay area. This young man wasn't particularly encouraged to come on board, and was actually leaving the hospice when he ran into a young doctor on his way out. The doctor asked where he was going, and the youth explained that he'd come to volunteer, but now wasn't so sure that was a good idea. "What do you love to do?" the doctor asked him, and the young man told him that he liked to make home movies. So the canny doctor invited him to give it a try on the hospice ward.

Before anyone quite knew what was happening, the kid started videotaping patients, asking them where they'd like to go if they could leave hospice. One said the beach; another mentioned a local bar; a third wished he could visit his old house. So the young man went to the beach, and filmed waves rolling in and out. He filmed the dying woman's favorite bar, ordering her usual drink—a Mai Tai. He even managed to talk his way into and film the last patient's former house, though it was already occupied by others. Finally, he came back to the hospice and gave a film festival, attended by patients and caregivers. Frank said everybody had a great time, even if the videos were a little bit funky.

When my own father began to experience active dying, my sister, her children, and I were invited to listen to a rapid account of his life. He had never talked about his war experiences, and now was the time. He seemed to be finally letting go of memories that had haunted him for sixty years. He also regaled us with his successes in business, and charmed us with stories of his love for our mother. We had to lean in and pay attention to keep up with him—it was like tracking his entire life on fast-forward.

We felt instinctively that he really wanted this opportunity to review his years, and we were genuinely interested. At one point, I'd been up all night with him and put my head down for a moment of rest—but within a few minutes, he insisted that I wake up and be there for his final stories, bless him. Though weary, I was delighted that he could finally tell us what he really needed from us, and that we could be there for him. We listened as he summed up a life lived with love, energy, and integrity. He seemed to know, perhaps for the first time, how much he had given and loved, and we could all feel it along with him.

Our listening offered him the chance to discover meaning in recalling his history, resolve feelings, and open up a sense of purpose in the experience of dying. But, mysteriously and powerfully, his telling helped us as well. In the circle of intense intimacy around his bed, the kids, my sister, and I were brought to a great sense of love and appreciation for him and each other through his presence and his words. When he had no more energy, he grew quiet, then slipped into silence until near his death.

Again and again, in this miraculous work with death, we see how that which ostensibly helps the one who dies also has the most profound and lasting benefit for survivors. When we show up to serve, when we are present for a dying one's stories or life summary, that great heart of compassion as wide as the whole world is summoned and can grow between us and bless us.

I felt this tender heart in myself as my father was actively dying. I did not work for it or call it up; it wasn't any special ability on my part. Rather, it was spontaneously pressed into service at the moment of his most acute suffering. As I sat with him during his last night, his arms bruised and scraped from flailing, blood streaming from his mouth from biting his lips and tongue, I could only hold him and thank him, again and again, for all the love he had shown me. What comfort I gave him was simply boundless gratitude. I could find no other words. Just the repetition of words of thanks and gratitude that carried us both through that terrible thrashing that comes before the final peace of death.

As I held his head and whispered into his ear, it wasn't me speaking, but the heart of the world. I only realized this much later; at the time, I had no thoughts, just the welling of a broken and grateful heart. And it is out of this very brokenness, paradoxically, that we can begin to sew that whole cloth of completion, finding meaning in suffering or in the small, simple moments of connection, whenever we allow ourselves to show up for them completely.

# MEDITATION

## *Letting Go through the Breath*

Let your body settle as you shift and settle into your relaxed, stable sitting posture. Strong back, soft front. Remember why you are meditating. Cultivate a heart of kindness and altruism.

Bring your attention gently to your breath. Allow yourself to breathe naturally and comfortably. Be aware of the breath moving in and out of your nose.

Bring your attention to the touch of your breath on the nose, where the breath enters. Gently keep your attention at this point. If you lose touch with this point of attention, when you realize that you have strayed, bring your mind back to the breath.

Thoughts, feelings, and sensations arise as you are breathing. This is natural. They are like waves on a beach or leaves falling. No need to grasp or identify with these phenomena. Accept that this is happening and keep your foreground attention on the breath.

Be aware of the quality of your breaths. Are they long or short, shallow or deep? Let your mind touch and be aware of the quality of your breath as you keep your foreground attention on the point where the breath enters the nose.

Be with each moment as it is. Don't try to do anything or get anything from this experience. Simply accept whatever is arising and let your attention rest on your breath.

Let your attention penetrate to the experience of the sensation of breathing. If thoughts arise, simply be aware of their presence and motion in the mind, and return to the breath. Do not invite your thoughts to tea. Just let thoughts arise and pass away.

The same goes for feelings and sensations—moment by moment, thoughts, feelings, and sensations arise in our experience. Then they pass from our experience. Let them arise and pass away into emptiness. There is no need to do anything but keep your attention gently on your breath.

Who we feel we are also arises from emptiness and will pass away into emptiness. Do not cling to any idea or description. Let go of the sense of a solid identity and be with the flow of your breath.

All things in our experience, whether the body or in the mind or the world, arise and pass away. Simply keep your attention gently on the flow of the breath, and let be the arising, abiding, and passing of phenomena, including your own life.

# 15

## Between Life, Between People

### *How We Forgive, Reconcile, Express Gratitude, and Love*

A s Donald lay dying of lung cancer, he asked to speak with his father. These two men had neither met nor spoken to each other for many years. Donald had left home at a young age because his father was an alcoholic and had physically abused him. Close to death, Donald realized that the abuse was in the distant past, and he suddenly understood that his father had also suffered. Donald felt that he had to reconcile with his father now or never.

It's strange—all of our lives, our innate wisdom tells us to let go, to relax, and to relinquish fearful efforts to control. But our cultural conditioning and our personal history caution us to hold on to people, experiences, and accomplishments. "Never let go of anything—that's the way to be happy," the voices whisper—or sometimes scream. And so we spend our entire lives in a battle between that deep inner wisdom and the culture's message about clinging and control. Being with dying is above all the time to turn to trust, and rest in the voice of truth within.

Forgiveness, one form of surrendering, often becomes especially meaningful as death nears. When Donald knew he didn't have much time, suddenly reconciliation took on a looming importance. He and his father did meet again, after decades of silence, and later Donald told a close friend that their encounter was about more than forgiveness; he used the word *redemption* to describe the brief time they spent together.

Fostering this kind of forgiveness can be an intensely poignant experience, calling for trust and presence. As caregivers, we may be asked to be the bridge between long-separated shores of blame and misunderstanding, and help mend the sense of brokenness that has awakened with anticipated loss. Perhaps influenced by our calm acceptance of things as they are, the dying person may find a way to forgive and let go of long-held anger and sadness. Forgiving can make a significant difference to everyone, including survivors and their experience of grieving.

Along with expressing gratitude and love, making a space for forgiveness and reconciliation can help transform sadness, regret, anger, and disappointment; these actions, centered around relationship, often make it easier for the dying one to let go of any remaining fear, anxiety, restlessness, or sense of failure and incompleteness with regard to his or her family, friends, and loved ones.

Interestingly, most of us think we will have time before we die to take care of our lapsed relationships, heal old wounds, and make peace with those around us. Yet how do we know we won't die a sudden death, without time to fulfill these tasks? Who knows if we will even know who we are when we are nearing death, should you or I have dementia or Alzheimer's. Remember the nine contemplations, and death's inevitability; its timing is completely uncertain, and recollecting this truth can help us reorder our priorities. A later contemplation in the series reminds us that we cannot know what will be the cause of our death. Taking care of our relationships along the way might not be such a bad thing to do. If we don't die a sudden death, and are sufficiently cogent and emotionally present, then perhaps we will be fortunate enough to forgive and offer love. But thinking about these tasks now reminds us not to wait to live a more loving life, less a process of regrets and more an experience of completion, even celebration. Best to appreciate our lives and our precious relationships right now, while we still can!

If the dying one has time, however, her caregivers can support her in setting her interpersonal affairs in order. So many times the survivors are left with a sense of unfinished business haunting them, wounds that take a long time to heal and prolong grief, turning the daily taste of life sour and bitter. And then having a chance to heal any betrayals, to forgive and to be forgiven, makes it easier for the dying one to let go and relax into spaciousness without hindrance.

Many spiritual traditions say that the last thoughts of a dying person have deep significance. If we attend to forgiveness, we can more easily be with the good events of a person's life, reminding her of the beneficial aspects of the past—such as the people she has loved and the gratitude she feels for them—helping her to gentle her state of mind and find peace. Recalling her most worthwhile connections may help relax and open the dying one's horizon, nurturing a greater sense of clarity and worth, making dying less of a struggle or an experience marked by regret.

Other interpersonal tasks of dying are subtler, and may be less intuitive for caregivers. One aspect to approach without too much attachment is who the patient wishes to be present for his death.

Surprisingly often, people die while their caregivers have left the room; I imagine they simply want to die peacefully, and alone. How many times have I seen the dying person wait until everyone is out of the room to let go! Maybe this person wants to be free of all that attention that keeps her in life. Some people want their family not to be there because they feel such a strong attachment, positive or negative, to family members. Maybe they feel, and perhaps rightly so, that the family would prevent them from a graceful release, and that it is easier to die among compassionate strangers, or alone. If this is the case, the family will usually need a great deal of support to accept this decision.

One man felt that his family couldn't bear to take care of him as he was dying of AIDS. When they visited him, he felt agitated and exhausted by their presence, and they were distraught by the bleakness of his condition. I quietly shared with them that I thought he was gradually letting go of his life and all that he cared about, including them. Their son felt grateful to have the opportunity to say goodbye, but he didn't want them to suffer as he went through the slow dissolving of his body. He could let go more easily with those who were not his family. His family understood, seemed relieved, and backed away, finding other ways to deal with their anticipatory grief.

Some people want to be held when they die, like Issan, who died in the arms of his good friend. Other people do not want to be touched; they want the caregiver just to be present. Some people will wait until caregivers leave the room, because dying alone is what they need to do. Some people want the whole family there, like the young Afro-American man dying of renal failure whose family surrounded his hospital bed singing gospel as he lapsed into a terminal delirium. Some people want total control over the process; "no help wanted, please." Some people need to be talked through their dying: "I will go with you as far as I can go," said a caregiver to her dying charge. Some people desire the grace and freedom of deep silence.

Interpersonal tasks often hinge on cultural differences, and cross-cultural sensitivity must be cultivated as we work with dying people and communities from cultures other than our own. There are so many differing customs, culturally determined needs, perceptions of illness and death, interventions, gender and age issues, nuances of the caregiver/patient relationship, belief systems, and religious and spiritual practices that shape our relationship to the community. We can easily offend others without realizing it by violating culturally determined boundaries and personal preferences. And the dying one may be reconciling with his cultural background as much as with family members.

I am grateful for the many prescriptions for being with dying that have been given to me over the years. Yet when actually sitting with a dying person, I have to put all these wonderful teachings aside, settle down with the breath, and let myself be guided by the truth of the moment. In letting the one who is dying take the lead, she will let us know one way or another what is appropriate for her, who she needs to have nearby, and with whom she needs to make her peace and express her deepest, most intimate feelings of gratitude and love.

## MEDITATION

*Boundless Abodes for Transforming Relationships*

With the following boundless abodes, choose phrases that are personally meaningful to you and use them in your practice. You can alter them in any way you wish or create your own. Remember, too, that the practices can also be used by caregivers.

To begin, find as comfortable a position as possible, sitting or lying down. Take a few deep breaths to let your body settle. Bring your attention to your breath and begin to say your chosen phrase silently in rhythm with the breath. You can also experiment with just having your attention settle on the phrase without the anchor of the breath. Feel the meaning of what you are saying, without trying or forcing anything.

- May I be open with others and myself about my dying.
- May I receive others' love and compassion.
- May I forgive myself for mistakes made and things left undone.
- May all those whom I have harmed forgive me, and may I forgive those who have harmed me.
- May kindness sustain my caregivers and me.
- May I, and all beings, live and die peacefully.

# 16

## The Great Matter

### *There Is No One Right Way*

ONCE, A young Zen student was walking through the streets of Kyoto when he heard someone screaming. He ran toward the sound as quickly as he could, and was stunned to find his teacher being beaten to death by robbers. There was nothing he could do; the robbers fled and his teacher died before his eyes.

The student was not only horrified by his teacher's death, but also by the fact that his supposedly enlightened master had died screaming. He became morbidly depressed, until his next teacher finally asked him what was wrong. He poured out the whole story, expecting his new teacher to be disapproving as well. But to his surprise, the teacher nodded. It is only natural, he told the student, to cry out when being beaten to death!

We have already looked at some common responses to dying: fearing death, denying death, grieving death, defying death, accepting death, and liberating death. But there is such wide variability in how people relate to their dying, sometimes shifting rapidly from moment to moment. Our job in being with dying is to accept even the most unaccepting and unacceptable approaches to death and realize that they are normal too, just like the Zen master who died screaming. We call this "the waves of birth and death." Our challenge is to learn not to drown in those waves but to ride them freely. Dying involves intense psycho-spiritual experiences, some of which may be pleasant and even inspiring, and some very unpleasant. When the dying one hits a wall, we must be prepared to work with the hard, raw, gritty aspects of dying, such as pain, obsessive suffering, denial, negative (and positive) transference, depression, anger, blame, shame, judgmental mind, hallucinations and visions, confusion, pain, fear, grief, including anticipatory grief, and loss. These experiences are really accepting death as the ultimate moment of life, and realizing somehow that the low-tide experiences are where we learn.

The path dying follows often does not conform to our expectations. I knew a hospice nurse who sat with her mother at home as she was dying. Although her mother had always been a cheerful person, as she neared death, she grew more and more angry. When she began to scream in anger, her daughter was deeply shaken. But in the core of her being, she felt that she should simply bear witness to her mother's rage, without responding. At the end of four miserable days, her mother suddenly relaxed, smiled, and died peacefully.

This nurse told me later that her mother would have been medicated out of her anger had she been in an institution. Although she felt more than a little uncertain about allowing her mother's extreme expression of rage, in retrospect she felt that it was rage that had been pent up for her entire lifetime. The look of relief and release on her mother's face as she died was all her daughter needed to see in order to know she had done the best thing for both of them.

Sometimes dying people will go through intense suffering and wake up feeling redeemed. A dying person may experience distressing mental states, including anger, aggression, inflation, mania, depression, and delusion. We are asked to be there for it all. These mental experiences sometimes get "managed" as problems, and the dying person treated as suffering a psychological crisis. But many of us have learned that these experiences are a normal part of dying. They are often enough a territory in the geography of dying, and in some cases, can even be beneficial. We are usually the ones unable to tolerate these unusual experiences, and it's often rattled, frightened family members or friends who insist on medicating the dying person. At other times, of course, medication may be helpful in shifting the suffering. Try to ascertain what is best for the dying person. Let her take the lead in her own death.

Earlier I shared my correspondence with Steven, who died of a lung disease. The following is a letter from his physician, who was a participant in our professional training program for clinicians:

> As with everything he did in his life, Steven went out fighting. By the last day, he required continuous oxygen. When his breathing became terribly labored (and long after he had become unresponsive), we turned off the oxygen. I fully expected him to pass in minutes. No, not Steven. Never the easy way out. He still labored, minutes turning into hours. Family and friends started reading poetry—Blake, Wordsworth—preparing for a night that seemed to have no end. At one point, I thought of co-meditation, but couldn't imagine how I could do that. Too late now, I thought. Then, without any idea what I was doing, and with still no end in his agony in immediate sight, I began speaking into his ear, my forehead almost resting on his, my hand slowly rubbing his chest in soft circles, as I whispered to him to relax, to slow the breath down, to be easy. Within minutes his breathing pattern slowed, the labored quality going. A few minutes later, when it had slowed even more, the end clearly near, I called someone else over to take my place by his side, and with her now whispering in his ear, he died quietly, peacefully. A long, hard labor over. The night complete. A man reborn into another world.

Over the years, I have asked many professional caregivers if they have witnessed an agonizing moment of death. Very few have answered yes, noting that in their overall experience such a moment was an exception. The task can be completed even after a struggle during active dying, for ultimately human beings seem quite well designed to die. Our mental faculties tend to unbind before the body releases itself. But there is often resistance as active dying is entered, a chaotic phase of the journey that can be dismaying for those who must witness it. This is when we lean hardest for support on our tenets of not-knowing and bearing witness to whatever is, just as it is.

Not-knowing and bearing witness have long been my refuges and guides in being with dying, though I did not use these words to describe how I worked with the encounter with death. In the 1980s, I spent several years traveling back and forth to Seattle from Southern California to be with John and Kenny, both of whom had AIDS. John died first, and all our loving of him, all our holding of him, all the support offered to him, seemed to do little good. He just suffered and then suffered some more. Till the very end, he could not believe he was actually dying. Eventually he developed dementia and lost his mind. He died a hard death—hard for him and hard for those of us near to him. I learned that sometimes all we can do is just be present. We are powerless to change the tide of suffering, dying, and death.

After his partner's death Kenny moved to a tiny room in a brownstone in the Bronx. Whenever I went to New York, I'd go to see him. Sitting by his bed, I would listen to his quiet request that I help him die. I could understand why Kenny wanted to take his life. It seemed to him that he had little to live for. He was alone most of the time in a tiny sweltering room in a desolate corner of New York, with few visitors and little support. I invited Kenny to move in with me, but he declined, saying he wanted to stay on the East Coast near his sister. In the end, I had very little to give Kenny except for presence. We meditated together, and we shared moments of deep peace. Then one evening Kenny said to me, "You know, it's October now. In November I'm going to my sister's farm and put myself on the earth and die."

And that is exactly what he did. He chose the time of his death, and he took his own life. He took it peacefully, close to what he loved the most, the land he had tended since he was a child. I heard from those who were with him that it took him a long time to die, but that he was right there through all of it.

Being with dying often means bearing witness to and accepting the unbearable and the unacceptable. I was not comfortable with Kenny's decision to take his own life, but neither did I advise him against it. I hoped to give him something to live for; but later I sensed that the last act in his life might have been a way for Kenny to choose what he felt was right for him and those around him. His suffering was wrenching, and his natural death was near. He told his caregivers he wanted to be there for his dying. And although little of him was left as he died, it seemed he was able to be present as he cut the knot that bound him to this world.

As caregivers, we must be prepared to explore with dying people and their community issues related to quality of life, including the use of interventions attempting to prolong life and issues concerning hastened death. I believe that our own beliefs and feelings about these issues are not what is important. We must create trust and make it safe for people to explore and discuss these matters openly. It's especially crucial to explain what advance directives entail and how to set them up. We want people to know realistically about the possible outcomes of resuscitation or the use of extreme interventions, and to help people be prepared for both the best and the worst. We also want to have prepared the family and community by creating an atmosphere of trust, and whatever they choose, we want to support our dying loved one as tenderly and with as much equanimity as possible, that combination of the strong back and soft front, the iron man and the wooden puppet.

Another story, like Kenny's, entered my life, when several years ago, an older woman asked that we support her as she was dying of a rare neurological disorder. After some months, she disclosed that she did not want to continue living with her rapidly decreasing capacities and her increasing pain. Over the months we gently and firmly tried to find ways to offer her greater love and support. But she was determined to end her life.

She tried more than once to end her life, but did not succeed. Each time she swallowed the pills, her partner would call 911 and a rescue team would arrive and resuscitate her. Her anger at these rescues was raw, as she had been in a psychiatric institution as a young woman and felt a deep fury that others were controlling her destiny. It was not a matter of love and reason being an intervention to end this cycle of misery. All the spiritual and practical issues meant nothing to her in the face of her history.

Our team reluctantly told her that we could not support her suicide, although we loved and respected her. We were legally bound to "call for help." At this, she and her partner agreed to not inform us or anyone if she attempted suicide again, and in this way, they would let things take their course. Knowing these two, I imagine this was a hard decision; nor was ours an easy one either.

One Wednesday morning, the phone rang. Our friend had attempted suicide. This time she went comatose and had entered a vegetative state. When they called me, she had been that way for four days. I immediately drove to her house to find her unconscious and completely chaotic, her breathing ragged, her body tossing about like flotsam in stormy waves.

The hospice nurse and my assistant, who knew her well, asked that I spend some time alone with her. "She would want this," they said. I sat down beside the bed and took her hands in mine. Her eyes were blank, her body twisting and sweating profusely. I began breathing with her, telling her that she was loved and that it was OK for her to let go. We breathed together, and gradually, almost imperceptibly, with me quietly saying "yes" on her out-breath, her breathing slowed and became lighter and lighter, until at last she slipped away and was gone.

Sometimes all that a loved one dying a difficult death needs is permission to leave, and the knowledge that they have been loved. Prayers, practices of devotion, and blessings from teachers, relatives, and friends can be helpful in transforming the atmosphere. One friend's father struggled in active dying until she told him, "Death is safe; death is safe," quoting consciousness pioneer Ram Dass. Her father clung to the phrase like a lifeline and repeated it until his last breath, using it as a raft to carry him to the other shore.

Another caregiver used the Lord's Prayer as her raft, during the night-long vigil she kept by the bedside of her mother. I myself have floated on the Heart Sutra, chanting it softly under my breath. And how often have we heard family members encourage their dying relative, "Move toward the light," "It is all right to die," "We are here with you," "You are loved and can let go," or even, simply, "Thank you for all you have done for us." In my father's final hours, I could only thank him repeatedly for all he had done for me and for so many. Simple gratitude can hold our hands tightly in the very darkest moments, if we can manage to stay upright in the storm.

To illustrate surrender in dying, Henri Nouwen used the story of a trapeze artist who told a secret: that the important person to watch is the one who catches the other, not the one who jumps from the trapeze into the arms of the catcher. "The catcher," said Nouwen, "is the real star. . . . [T]he flyer does nothing and the catcher does everything. . . . The flyer must trust, with outstretched arms, that his catcher will be there for him."* I think also of Christ's dying words, in the Gospel of Luke: "Father, into your hands I commend my spirit." Prayers and good words can carry us across, but there is a moment when we must leap, trusting the other side will catch and hold us safely.

We need to learn to stay with suffering without trying to change it or fix it. Only when we are able to be present for our own suffering are we able to be present for the suffering of others, and the difficulties they may encounter in dying. The practice of insight meditation, in which we watch the ebb and flow of mental activity, is a good way to cultivate this ability. With gentle precision and honesty, we stay with our experience through foul weather and clear skies. Seeing the mental weather go through its changes gives us some sense of the nature and cause of our suffering and also of the possibility that, at the very ground of our being, we are all free from suffering.

The great Zen teacher Dainin Katagiri Roshi knew this. When he was diagnosed with terminal cancer, his students came from far and wide to be with him and help—but they were also frightened and confused at the thought that their teacher was subject to ordinary human frailty. One day he called his students to his bedside, and said, "I see you are watching me closely; you want to see how a Zen master dies. I'll show you." Katagiri kicked his legs wildly and flailed his arms in alarm, crying out, "I don't want to die! I don't want to die!" Then he stopped, and looked at them. "I don't know how I will die. Maybe I will die in fear or pain. Remember, there is no right way."

---

* Henri Nouwen, *Our Greatest Gift: A Meditation on Dying and Caring* (San Francisco: HarperCollins, 1995), 67.

When we cultivate our ability to be present, we train our hearts to open to suffering, transforming it into well-being and offering our own natural mercy. We're asked to invite suffering into our being and let it break open the armor of our heart. The tender spaciousness that arises awakens selfless warmth and compassion. We cannot help but send our love and kindness to the one who is suffering, be it others or ourselves.

It is both true that suffering exists, and that some deaths are challenging—and it is also true that beings can be free of suffering and that death can be natural and simple. When I sit with a dying person, I must perceive both of these dimensions together. I must look from a place in myself that includes suffering but that is bigger than suffering. I must look from a heart that is so big that it is open to everything, including freedom from suffering. Can I see her struggling to die and her great heart as well? Can I see his true nature, who he really is, deeper than the story?

I sat once with a woman who felt completely defeated by her critical dying mother. From her mother's point of view, she could do nothing right. The heaviness of failure shrank her body until it seemed small and defended. I shared with her how much effort it took to let go of my own expectations. This woman wanted her mother's death to be "good" and her work to be easy. But in the end, her practice was to let go, again and again, of her expectations, her desire to flee, and her sense of despair. This required diligence, perseverance, and a pretty good sense of humor. But before she could start to let go of her own suffering, she also had to accept that it was completely real.

Ultimately, to help others, we must relate with kindness toward our own rage, helplessness, and frustration, our doubt, bitterness, and fear. We must get in touch with the obstacles that prevent us from understanding and caring. Through accepting our own suffering, we can begin to be with others in a more open, kind, and understanding way. We learn not to reject difficult situations or people. Rather, we meet them exactly where they are.

This is the basis for our work with the dying. We cannot prevent death from happening, or make it easier for the dying one to accept it. We *can* learn to meet it and find mercy in it. Cultivate the detail and the craft of this practice. It can be done on every breath that you take, every breath that you give. Our own difficult personal experiences become the bridge leading us to compassion and to giving no fear when the ones we love are struggling with difficult deaths. This is what the old teachers mean by their saying "riding the waves of birth and death."

# MEDITATION

## *Encountering Death*

### PART ONE: CO-MEDITATION

The following practice entails a simplified version of the body scan, shared breathing with emphasis on the out-breath, and finally a guided visualization. The practice can be done in the hospital or home. The most important element in the practice is the relationship of trust between the dying person and the caregiver. This practice was developed by Patricia Shelton and Richard Boerstler, and I adapted it further for our professional training program for caregivers.

When doing this with a dying person, it is important to have a second person there to take care of any needs that arise as the practice is unfolding.

Make sure that the atmosphere around the dying person is comfortable, secure, and quiet and that there will be no interruptions. Help the dying person find a comfortable position that he or she will be able to sustain for up to an hour.

Explain the practice to the dying person. ("This is a way that we can meditate together. It will involve several relaxation exercises and a guided visualization. I hope you will be able to let go and be helped by what we are doing.") The practice is calibrated to the needs and situation of the dying person. The light should be low and the dying person covered up so he or she is comfortable.

The caregiver then does a simple version of the body scan with the dying person, beginning with the head.

The practice can be done lying down, sitting on a practice cushion, or sitting on a chair:

Let your body relax and soften. Bring your attention to your breath. Breathe deeply into your belly. Feel your whole body beginning to settle.

Breathing deeply, bring your awareness to the top part of your head, to your skull and scalp. Breathe into your scalp. As thoughts arise, just let them be. Be aware of any tension in your scalp. On your next inhalation, give space to whatever you experience.

Move your attention to your forehead. Be aware of your forehead, accepting whatever tension might be there. Breathe into your temples. Accept any tension or pain in your temples. As you breathe out, accept whatever you are experiencing.

If you can, put your hand over your eyes as you breathe into them. Be aware of how your eyes feel. See if you can soften your eyes as you breathe in. As you breathe out, let go of all hardness in and around your eyes.

Breathe in through your nose. Feel air passing in and out of your nostrils. On your next inhalation bring your awareness to the feeling of cool air entering. Feel the exhalation passing out of your nostrils.

Gently move your awareness to your throat and neck. Breathe into this area, accepting whatever tightness you might feel. As you exhale, rest lightly with your experience.

Shift your awareness as you breathe into your shoulders. Be aware of any sense of heaviness. On your in-breath give your shoulders space. On your out-breath drop them down easily.

Let your awareness be in your arms, inhaling and exhaling into them. How do they feel? Be aware of any tightness. There is nothing that you need to hold on to. Touch your hands with awareness. Let them open, palms facing upward. Breathe into the palms of your hands.

Your awareness is in your spine. Breathe into your spine, letting it stretch with your in-breath, aware of your rib cage expanding. As you exhale, feel your spine lengthen.

Bring your attention to your chest and lungs. Breathe as

deeply into your lungs as you are able, and fill them so that your chest rises after your belly does. Give your chest space in which to breathe deeply. Breathing in, feel your chest opening, your lungs expanding. Be aware of any tightness or feelings of loss and sorrow. This is a very deep breath.

Now breathe into your heart. Be aware of openness or tightness in and around your heart. Bring your attention to your diaphragm. Does your diaphragm open as you breathe in deeply? Breathing in, feel your diaphragm, giving your heart and lungs space in which to expand. Be aware of your whole torso as you exhale.

Bring your attention to your stomach. As you inhale, feel your guts expanding with the in-breath. On your out-breath be aware of any tension in your digestive system. Be aware of the function of elimination performed by your bowels and bladder. Breathing in, appreciate your reproductive organs. Exhaling, give the entire pelvic area a feeling of space and ease.

Be aware of your legs and knees. Breathe into your thighs as you settle your attention into them. Breathing out, let your thighs soften. On your inhalation feel gratitude for the support of your legs. Breathing out, appreciate your legs, which have taken you so far in life. Breathe into your knees. On the out-breath be aware of the small muscles around your knees. Breathe in healing to them, and breathe out any tension and pain.

Breathe into your feet, bringing all your attention to your feet. On your out-breath, be aware of any tension. Imagine on your in-breath that you are breathing all the way through your body into your feet.

To complete this practice, slowly and smoothly bring your awareness from your feet to your legs; to your stomach and pelvic area; to your chest, heart, and lungs; to your spine; to your shoulders, arms, and hands; to your neck; to your face; to the top of your head. Breathe in and out smoothly as your awareness travels up and through your body.

When you have reached the top of your head, return your awareness to your breath, then let it gently spread to your whole body. Stay this way for some minutes. Take a few moments to relax with an open and quiet mind.

When the dying person is ready, the caregiver breathes gently and quietly with the dying person. When the caregiver feels it is an appropriate time, he or she breathes quietly and audibly the syllable *ah* on the out-breath of the dying person. The caregiver does this for five to ten minutes with the dying person, so the one who is dying can really bring her or his attention to the out-breath. If the dying person wishes, she or he may also say *ah* on the out-breath. The sound should be soft, almost like a yawn; the feeling is of surrender, of letting go.

When the dying person is deeply relaxed, the caregiver softly suggests that there be a short period of silence. Then the caregiver may say a prayer that is favored by the dying person or give a guided visualization on light. For example, the caregiver might suggest the dying person visualize a boundless ocean of light; then the caregiver guides the dying person to merge with or dissolve into the luminosity.

The session can finish with a dedication of the merit, a deep thanks, or a period of silent meditation. Sometimes it can be helpful for the caregiver to ask the dying person how he or she responded to the experience.

## PART TWO: BOUNDLESS ABODES FOR DYING

These are boundless abodes that a dying person can practice.

- May I accept my anger, fear, and sadness, knowing that my heart is not limited by these feelings.
- May all those I leave behind be safe and peaceful.
- May I remember my consciousness is much vaster than this body as I let go of this body.
- May I be open to the unknown as I leave behind the unknown.
- May I live and die in ease.

# 17

## The Broken Pine Branch
### *Deaths of Acceptance and Liberation*

D EAN HAD colon cancer, and he was in the final stages of dying. His kidneys were failing. As he seemed to be taking his last breaths, his family gathered by his bedside. In the final moment, though, doctors hauled him onto a gurney and rushed down the hall for an emergency procedure to resuscitate him. The family was in a state of shock—as was Dean, brought back from death's door.

At first he was angry that he was still alive; then he realized that he had experienced something very extraordinary. In the midst of his near-death experience, Dean had a piercing insight into the meaning of life and death—even his suffering had meaning. Though he lived only a few more days, those days were filled with a kind of inexplicable gratitude for the experience.

Some dying people will, at the end, discover death to be a mystery that cannot be explained in simply biological terms, and thus transform their fear of death into clear awareness and love. Others will complete the last and most precious task, that of realizing death as the ultimate moment of liberation from suffering, coming home to their original dwelling place, the luminous and clear nature of our mind and heart, now and at the moment of biological death.

The most inspiring, tender, and instructive deaths that I have known have been those of individuals whose whole lives had been spent cultivating inner awareness. Several Buddhist teachers who have died during my lifetime have given me a sense of what might be possible for you and me. Though riddled with cancer, His Holiness the Sixteenth Karmapa upheld his practice and equanimity throughout his dying. The Venerable Kalu Rinpoche and His Holiness Khyentse Rinpoche both assumed the meditation posture as they died. And Issan Dorsey kept serving his brothers who had AIDS even he was dying from the same disease.

A developed meditation practice can be the most powerful of all supports for a dying person. A mind that is clear and peaceful, even one that has disappeared into the well of Alzheimer's, can be a liberation for all. In Zen, when we sew our layperson's robes, we always embroider a broken pine branch in green thread on the back of the robe, right where it rests on the tender nape of the neck. This broken branch symbolizes the wholeness that can only come about when we have been completely broken open.

Francisco was dying of liver cancer. Shortly before he died, he heard the voice of his Tibetan Buddhist teacher over the phone admonishing him to clear his mind. Although he was a scientist, Cisco had also dedicated his adult life to Buddhist practice. Now was the greatest opportunity to bring practice to bear on the experience of liberation, said his teacher. Cisco asked his family to keep things very simple around him. His wife reported that she felt her husband dedicated his few remaining days to practice as he rested in a quiet interior state. He died peacefully a few days after hearing his teacher's words, with his wife lying beside him.

A spiritual outlook is integral to our realizing the developmental task of transcendence that is possible at death. It is important for dying people, family members, and friends—as well as health care providers—to recognize this and foster it if possible. In the hospital setting there is often resistance to pastoral or spiritual care of dying people. Those who provide such care are seen as not adding to the bottom line, or they are seen as doing "light" work, whereas the "real" work is medical. What conventional heath care institutions have often failed to realize is that spiritual care can reduce fear, stress, the need for certain medications and expensive interventions, lawsuits, and the time doctors and nurses must spend reassuring people. It can also benefit professional and family caregivers in helping them to come to terms with suffering, death, loss, and grief. The greatest treasure in this work with dying is attending to the spiritual dimension.

Some spiritual traditions teach that there is a deep level of the mind that stays intact at the moment of death and perhaps afterward. Although I personally cannot attest to what happens at the moment of death, my approach is to cover my back, in the event that consciousness continues following the death of the body. In case this happens, I want my mind and heart clear in order to meet the situation of transition. Since the meditation practices that foster this element of clarity also bring strength into one's daily life, why not?

I am reminded of a story about the Chinese Zen ancestor Hui Neng. He told his disciples to gather around him, as he had decided to "leave in the eighth month." His monks wept bitterly when they heard of his impending death. Hui Neng, honest and tough as ever, asked them whom they were crying for. Were they worried that he didn't know where he was going? Hui Neng said that, if he didn't know where he was headed, then he could not leave them like that. Instead, he said that what they were really crying about was that they themselves didn't know! If they knew, they would not cry, for true nature is without birth and death.

Often a dying person needs nothing but simplicity. A big sky and a quiet room can give peace. As one man lay dying, he asked that his bed be put next to a large window. Every day he would gaze into the blue sky of New Mexico. He told me one day that he was becoming that sky. He asked that no visitors bother him. He wanted to be quiet and alone with his sky. One morning he died peacefully facing his friend the big open sky, transcending his limited body.

Another man, brain tumor and all, got up from his deathbed, went to the door of his house, and looked expectantly at the road nearby. Although he had been withdrawn and noncommunicative for days, he said with complete clarity, "Let's go." And he did that night.

Recently, my friend Maggie was looking at a book of photographs of Tibet's holy Mount Kailash. An experienced practitioner of Tibetan

Buddhism, her greatest wish had been to go to Kailash. Renowned photographer Thomas Kelly was holding his book of remarkable photographs for her when he turned the page to the "inner *kora*" of Kailash—the most sacred and inaccessible of the pilgrims' paths. Maggie said one sentence, "Oh, if I did that I would surely die." Then suddenly her head fell into the book onto the photo of the high Kailash's stupas, and she in fact did die. Yes, that sounds quite unbelievable, but I heard this story from Tom shortly after Maggie died.

Laced through the process of slower dying are experiences that are rehearsals for the actual moment of death. A near-death or clinical-death experience can be profoundly beneficial in preparing an individual for the reality of death itself—like Dean's resuscitation. Often these visionary experiences are characterized by positive feelings that bring a dying person into a whole new relationship to his last days.

And dying evokes so many different kinds of experiences. When we are dying, we often experience an altered state of consciousness. Our body is changing, and with it our mind. We can have blissful or unpleasant mental experiences in the process. We can encounter loved ones who have died, relive good and bad memories, or have various kinds of hallucinations that are related to the medicines we are taking, to autointoxication, or simply to the mental transformations that happen in the dying process.

Nathaniel, an elderly man with whom I worked, took a medication for incontinence. Often at night he would awaken and hallucinate that food was in his bed. Sometimes it was sticky candy; one time it was lasagna, and another time, Cracker Jack. He would awaken his wife in the middle of the night and ask her what was going on with all this food. She assured him that there was no food in the bed, that he was dreaming. One day I asked Nathaniel if these experiences were pleasant, and he replied that it was always food that he liked to eat; it made him happy and reminded him of his childhood.

When Nathaniel stopped taking his medication, the hallucinations went away until he was near death, when they returned. Again, they were experiences of pleasure for him. Nathaniel had always loved food, and had lost his appetite as death drew near. Even though his last meal was invisible to everyone else, Nathaniel enjoyed it thoroughly.

During one of his hospitalizations, my father thought he was on a boat on the Myakka River in Florida. He was worried because he had no money with him. I suggested to him that where he was going, he might not need money after all. Giving me a big grin, he said, "You're right, kid. Thanks." Just before he died, he was miming eating something. My sister asked him what he was eating as he poured some imaginary food from his hand into his mouth. He said, "Peanuts." She asked how they tasted, and true to my dad's sense of humor, he responded, "Great, if they were real!"

What happens around the dying person is also sometimes surprisingly amusing. One becomes accustomed to the unexpected. Simone lay dying of congestive heart failure. On a ventilator, family and friends surrounding her and gently praying, her body was being mechanically breathed. I had been asked to come to sit with her and speak with her through the veil of near-death, offering her good words. After I left, a friend anointed her with oil and another put some holy ashes on her forehead. A little later, her bridge partner and close friend showed up, whipped his hankie out of his pocket, and wiped the "mess" off of his dying friend's face, not realizing that he was causing some dismay to those at the bedside. Their discomposure turned into soft, rolling chuckles, as this absurd moment was so typical of the dying woman's life.

Sometimes, in altered states of consciousness, people see deceased relatives, as was the case with my mother, who found herself on a cruise ship visiting the ports of her past and seeing her own mother and father along the way. A person can encounter spiritual figures, such as the Virgin Mary, angels, beings of light, or Buddha. Sometimes people have mystical experiences with insights about life that are profoundly enriching and give them a deep sense of purpose. Often these insights cannot be shared in words.

I sat once with a man dying of AIDS-related lymphoma. One afternoon, he asked me if I had seen a bird on the deck outside his bedroom. He said, "Do you see the bird? It's on the balcony. Can you see it?" I turned around and, of course, saw no bird. I asked, "What do you see?" He said, "It's the most beautiful white bird. Do you see? It's a huge dove."

He happily described this creature that seemed to be a kind of redeemer for him.

The deaths of the remarkable Buddhist teachers in all the schools of Buddhism remind us of our own potential to die awake. For example, the Chinese meditation master Hung-Chih Cheng-chüeh, left his mountain-top for the first time in thirty years. Dressed in his finest, he traveled to many places offering gratitude and farewell to students, patrons, government officials, and friends. Returning to his temple, he bathed, put on fresh robes, and gave a final talk to his disciples. He then requested that he be brought paper and brush. As soon as he had composed his death poem, he passed away, brush in hand.

For one caregiver I knew, the moments before her mother's death were truly a fulfillment of love and inspiration. Her mother had dedicated her life to community service and spiritual practice. She had made peace with her life and peace with her mind. Her last minutes on earth seemed to be filled with beauty. As she lay dying, she exclaimed quietly, "Beautiful, beautiful." She died with a smile on her face.

Some deaths are shockingly unexpected, like the man I mentioned who died on his meditation cushion on the first day of the retreat, or Maggie, who surprised us all. I heard recently about a young man who climbed the Grand Teton in Wyoming, who on his way home from this spectacular climb, felt ill, and thought he had altitude sickness. He immediately went to see his doctor, who discovered that he had leukemia. Early the next day, he suddenly died.

Although these deaths were utterly unexpected, they have a sense of strange beauty and symmetry about them. To be honest, I would rather die on the meditation cushion or after having seen or summited a noble mountain than in a car accident. But I also realize I don't really know how and when I will die.

There are also those who have been allowed to meet death after a long and careful preparation—as in the story of Julie. When I first met her, Julie's breast cancer had already metastasized into her liver, lungs, and brain. She was going blind, and her death wasn't far off. But Julie had a spirit that wouldn't quit, and she was determined to die with acceptance.

One day she invited me over. After we visited for a while, she asked, "Would you mind telling me how to die?"

I told her that what I might think I know is really just speculation. I am only a student of dying, not an expert. Then I suggested that we meditate together.

So we breathed together. I suggested to her, "When you breathe, let your attention be on your out-breath, because that will be your last breath indeed, that out-breath. When you let go of the out-breath, see how deeply you can let go into peacefulness. Think of it like this: Maybe you'll take another inhalation, and maybe not. For now, let most of your attention focus on breathing out."

The emphasis in our time together was on simplicity, clarity, and acceptance. We worked with giving attention to the out-breath and then later with a version of Zen teacher Thich Nhat Hanh's verse on mindful breathing: "In, out. Deep, slow. Calm, ease. Smile, release. Present moment, only moment." Each word or phrase supports inhalation and exhalation.

A few days later, fifteen women dealing with breast cancer came to spend the day practicing meditation with me. Most of these women had never sat in meditation before. Because her disease was so advanced, Julie's presence really disturbed some of those who considered themselves to be survivors. She looked like a Zen nun—no hair, black clothing. She had radiation burns on her neck, and her ears were transparent. She was also laughing.

At the end of most of our retreats, we sit in council to talk about our experiences. We pass a talking piece around the circle to honor each speaker and our connection to her, and everyone listens quietly and with concentration, as if it will be her last day on earth. And so it was that these women listened and spoke to one another. When it was Julie's turn to speak, she took the talking piece with both hands, saying, "I wish I could accept my death the way I accept this stick." She handed it back to the woman next to her and said, "Please let me accept the stick again." The stick was passed to her a second time. She was practicing accepting and letting go.

She spoke about her impending death with strength and optimism. She had done everything possible to keep herself alive, and now it was time to die. There was no self-pity. No regret. She was diamondlike in her clarity and tender in her truth. I felt such profound respect for her. I believe we all did. Some of us had worked closely with her during these months of struggle. She had cried hard with confusion that her efforts to cure her cancer had proven fruitless. She had fought to live, and now at last she was ready to die.

As her time drew nearer, Julie sat in another council with us for a whole day. One of the women in the group, Rebecca, was a nurse who felt despair that she could not bring compassion into the conventional hospital setting where she worked. Julie's turn to speak came soon after Rebecca's. All of us paid attention to the honesty and immediacy of her presence. I caught a glimpse of Rebecca, who gazed at Julie. She seemed to have forgotten her own frustration as she listened to the young woman talk.

In less than a week, Julie made good on her promise to die well. That council took place on a Wednesday. On Saturday Julie's grave was dug, and on Monday she was admitted to the same hospital where Rebecca worked. On Monday morning Rebecca walked into Room 201 and saw that Julie was her patient.

Later that morning, Rebecca asked Julie if she had signed a DNR (Do Not Resuscitate order). Julie had not, and when Rebecca told her what it was, Julie decided she wanted to sign the order. Knowing she was close to death, she wanted nothing to interfere with the natural sequence of her life.

At ten minutes to twelve that day, Julie told her friends, "I'm dying." And thirty minutes later she was gone. She died with the presence and support of her family, including her four brothers and mother. Also present were caregiver friends, as well as Rebecca and the hospital's patient advocate. They said it was a quiet and kind death, with a brief passing moment of fear that dissolved and settled down as her dying reached its end.

I came in half an hour later. People were tired, and they went to lunch. This gave me the opportunity to sit with Julie's body. Her right eye was closed, as though she were gazing inward. Her left eye was open, the pupil tiny as though she had been gazing into the light. Her mouth was slightly open, as though she had just said *ah*. In profile she looked as if she were in meditation. She didn't look asleep, but as if she had surrendered to peace.

Sitting with that body, I asked myself, Where did she go? Where has Julie gone? I couldn't imagine that the laughter I'd heard just a few days before was not still somehow present. I stayed with that question and then did some meditation practices intended for people who have just died.

In a short time the gurney rolled in, and Julie's body was lifted into a white plastic body bag. An entourage of nurses, family, friends, and the patient advocate took her down the hall as if she were royalty. She was then put into a station wagon and driven to a small village north of Santa Fe.

Julie had wanted a home burial. She had asked to be wrapped in an Indian blanket and put in the coffin that she had designed. She had worked with a furniture maker several weeks before to design her own coffin.

The next day her four elder brothers stepped into the gaping grave hole in a snowy field, receiving her coffin as if they were receiving her back into the earth. Then we all began to shovel dirt into the grave hole. It took a lot of work to fill up that hole. In the process I watched grief transform into community.

Julie's journey to the destination called death excluded nothing. She feared and she transformed fear, and in the end she gave no fear to others. Rather, she loved and in her dying drew others into love of one another. She planned and carried out her plan with dignity and bravery. She held nothing back, and finally nothing held her back. She was not sentimental; her mind and heart were fresh as she rested with not-knowing, her constant companion. She reminded me of the broken pine branch, which symbolizes the eternal and the fragile meeting in one thing. This is our life, a pine branch that is green and undying through the seasons and, at the same time, can be broken in any season.

Julie's brave acceptance of her death is not the same as resignation. Instead, she had the clear realization that death is part of life. One is reminded of Howard Auster, the writer Gore Vidal's longtime companion, turning in his wheelchair toward his illustrious friend and saying, "Well, it's been great," as the door to the operating room closes behind him, freeing not just one life but two.

In accepting death as inevitable, we don't label it as a good thing or a bad thing. As one of my teachers once said to me, "Death happens. It is just death, and how we meet it is up to us."

## MEDITATION

### *Dissolution of the Elements after Death*

The Tibetan Buddhist description of the dissolution of the elements is a map of the dying process that allows caregivers to familiarize themselves with the physical and mental signs of dying and the experience of death itself. It is also aimed at transforming the experience of dying, death, and rebirth into the experience of enlightenment and liberation. The practice that follows models a way for a practitioner to gain control over death, thus transcending death.

According to Tibetan Buddhism, when the foundations of our consciousness begin to collapse, we are in the process of dying. These foundations, in this system, refer to the so-called "winds," which control all forms of motion in the body, including talking, swallowing, spitting, urinating, defecating, movement of the limbs and joints, movement of the eyes, movement of the blood vessels, respiration, and digestion.

When the winds begin to transform in the process of dying, the mind goes through radical changes. An advanced yogi practices this deliberately, in order to gain control of all the mental states that arise in the process of dying and to experience death as the liberation it truly is.

The following description and practice of the dissolution of the elements arose over many centuries from the finely tuned observations of skilled meditators in Tibet. Although it is an esoteric practice, I have found it very helpful in working with dying people and caregivers. The practice confirms the observations that many professional caregivers have had of the physical, mental, and energetic changes in those who are dying. It has also been an aid, a map, and a source of inspiration to those who are actually going through or preparing to go through the experience of dying.

This description also includes the dissolving of the aspects of our subjec-

tive experience that give us a sense of an identity: the body, feelings, perceptions, mental formations, and capacity to discern. These same aspects affect
our experience of sickness and aging. When we have been ill, for example,
we can feel the body's heaviness and weakness, and recognize some of the
signs and symptoms described in the process. Or, as we age, the force of
gravity becomes more and more apparent. Our senses become less sensitive, and our grasp of the world lessens. So in both sickness and aging, we
are given a taste of what we will face as we are dying. Lamas have told me
that we also go through the dissolutions in the case of sudden death.

This particular practice involves the dissolution of not only the elements of mind but also the elements of body—earth, water, fire, air—and
then releasing into space. In releasing the elements of our identity that
compose what we know as "I," we allow ourselves to dissolve into radi-
ance, and ultimately to let go—or at least imagine letting go—of what we
know as our consciousness.

It is possible for dying people to use the text—whether they hear it read
or read it themselves—as a way to help familiarize themselves with dying
and to practice letting go. For example, one woman I cared for worked with
a recording of the text for a year before she died. According to her family,
she met her active dying with a remarkable absence of fear and resistance.

A powerful way to do this practice is to lie down in the "sleeping-lion
position," the position that the Buddha assumed when he was dying. Lie
on your right side, legs slightly drawn up. Your left arm rests along your
left side, and your right hand supports your head, with your hand holding your cheek. You may press your little finger against your right nostril
to complete the posture.

Make sure that you are comfortable, adjusting your position as needed
throughout the practice.

The top of your head is directed toward an image—real or visualized—
of your choice. This could be Jesus, the Buddha, Muhammad, Abraham,
Mary, or Quan Yin—any being who represents the essence of awakening,
compassion, love, and essential goodness. Your hope is that at your death
your consciousness will leave through the top of your head and manifest
as the essence of enlightenment.

Let the breath become even and smooth. Focus your attention on your breath. Whatever comes up—resistance or concern, grief or joy, boredom or story—notice and accept it, and return gently to the breath.

Imagine that this is an actual description of dying, of your dying. Notice what goes on as you do this practice. Let each of the feelings and sensations come up for you, pass through your mind and body, be noticed, and then released.

## 1. The Dissolution of Earth into Water and the Unbinding of the Body

Imagine that you are in your bed at home. Friends and family are around you, though you are barely aware of them. You are somewhat agitated, and you accept this state of mind.

Your body is weak. You do not have the energy to do anything but simply be here. You are letting go as you die. Feel your body becoming heavy, pressed down by a great weight. This heaviness is dense and deep, going right to the core of your body. Now your body feels as if it is dissolving, and your legs and arms don't feel as if they belong to your body. You feel as though you are slowly sinking in water, and deep weariness penetrates every cell of your body. Wake up as this body lets go.

Your senses are less attuned to the outside world. Your sight is dim. It is difficult to open and close your eyes. Your sensory grasp on the world is loosening. As your body slips away, the outside world is slipping away from you as well.

Your skin is pale as your blood pressure drops. The blood withdraws into the central part of your body. You are drowsy and weak, with no interest in the outside world. You sink deeper and deeper into a blurry, vague mental state. Whatever visions you see appear like blue mirages.

This is the dissolution of body and of our relationship to the physical world—these feelings of heaviness, drowsiness, being weighed down, the loss of definition, the withdrawal of color from our bodies, the loss of control, and our inability to see the form world around us.

In this state of mind and body, be awake and effortlessly present. The mind can be still and reflective as you let go. Be present as this body is dying. This body is not you. This is the dissolution of the element of earth as it sinks into water and as form unbinds into feelings.

## 2. THE DISSOLUTION OF THE WATER ELEMENT INTO FIRE AND THE UNBINDING OF FEELINGS

Feel your body dissolving. As you let go, your hearing is diminished, and you sink into a blurred state of mind.

Your nose is running; saliva is leaking out of your mouth. There is a watery discharge coming out of your eyes. It is difficult to hold your urine. Your skin is clammy.

As fluids leave the body, the body becomes parched. Your skin is papery. Your mouth is drawn, and your lips are chapped. Your tongue is thick, sticky, and heavy. Your throat is scratchy and clogged. Your nostrils seem to cave in, burning with dryness as you inhale. Your eyes feel sandy and sting. You are not passing much urine. You have a thirst that no amount of water can quench.

Let go fully into this dryness. Release the fluid element of your body, of water and of feeling.

Your mind is hazy, and you are irritable. You have ceased to experience pain, pleasure, or even indifference. You do not differentiate between physical and mental impressions. Those kinds of distinctions are not important to you now.

When you look behind your eyes, you see a vision of swirling smoke. The water element is dissolving into fire. This is the end of your responsiveness to phenomena. As you let go, wake up in this vision of swirling smoke.

## 3. THE DISSOLUTION OF THE FIRE ELEMENT INTO AIR AND THE UNBINDING OF PERCEPTIONS

As the fire element of your body begins to dissolve into air, your body feels cool. Heat withdraws from your feet and hands into the body's core. Your breath is cold as it passes through your mouth and nose. Your mouth, nose, and eyes dry out even more. Your ability to perceive is further diminished. The fire element is dissolving into the element of air.

You cannot smell anything. You are not hungry nor can you digest food. You cannot drink or swallow. The in-breath is less strong, and the out-breath is longer. Your mental perception alternates between lucidity and confusion. You cannot see, hear, taste, touch, or smell as the sense fields fade away. Your in-breath is short. Your out-breath is long.

You cannot remember the names of your loved ones, and you cannot recognize those around you. You have lost any sense of purpose in your life and have no interest in what is going on around you.

You may feel as though you were being consumed in a blaze of fire that rises into space. Let go into this fire as your mind releases itself. Or, you may see sparks, almost like fireflies. Wake up in this vision of shimmering sparks. This is the dissolution of the fire element into air and the unbinding of your ability to perceive.

## 4. The Dissolution of the Wind Element into Space and the Unbinding of Mental Formations

You have now given up any sense of volition. Accept this aimlessness free of meaning and purpose. Your in-breath is short; your out-breath is long. The mind is no longer aware of the outside world.

As the element of air dissolves, you have visions. These visions relate to who you are and how you have lived your life. You may see your family or your ancestors in a peaceful setting. You may see beautiful people, saints, or friends welcoming you. You may relive pleasant experiences from your past.

You may also have demonic visions. If you have hurt others, those whom you have injured may appear to you. Difficult moments of your life may arise to haunt you. You may see people with whom you have had negative interactions attacking you. You may even cry out in fear.

Do not identify with these visions. Simply let them be. The element of air is dissolving. You do not have to do anything. Just practice this breath of release and let go of everything.

Your tongue is thick and heavy; its root is blue. You have lost your taste for life as you lose the sense of taste. You cannot feel texture or body sensations. Your body is barely moving. The last energy of your body is withdrawing to your body's core. Whatever heat is left in your body now resides in the area of the heart. The in-breath is short, a mere sip of air. The out-breath is long and uneven. Your eyes, gazing into emptiness, roll upward. No intellect is present.

Your consciousness at this point is reduced to a smaller and smaller entity. After three rounds of respiration, your body lifts slightly to meet the breath, which does not enter. Mental functions cease altogether. Consciousness dissolves into space. The perception from the outside is that you are dead. Breathing and brain function have stopped. Know this empty state. Surrender to it. This is the element of wind dissolving into space.

At the moment of physical death, one sees a small, flickering flame like a candle. It is suddenly extinguished, and you are without awareness.

## 5. The Inner Dissolutions

From the crown a white drop is propelled by the inner winds downward through the central channel toward the heart. This is the male essence, and anger transforms into profound clarity. You experience an immaculate autumn sky filled with brilliant sunlight.

A red drop from the base of the spine is propelled upward through the central channel toward the heart. This is the female essence, and desire transforms into profound bliss. You experience a vast and clear copperred autumn sky of dusk.

The white and red drops meet in the heart and surround your consciousness. The winds enter your consciousness. You are now freed from the conceptual mind. Thick darkness like a deep autumn night sky appears. You dissolve into unconsciousness.

Out of this nothingness, luminescence arises. You are one with a clear dawn sky free of sunlight, moonlight, and darkness. You are bliss and clarity. Now the clear light of presence is liberated, the mother light of your awareness.

This is your ultimate great perfection.

This is the actual moment of death.

# 18

## Gratitude for the Vessel
### *Care of the Body after Death*

WHEN DAVID DIED of a brain tumor, he had already discussed his final wishes with his family, and they had been instructed how to take care of his body after his death. So as I arrived to help, twenty minutes after he had died, I found a calm and very moving scene of loving care taking place.

His partner was gently swabbing his mouth clean of mucus; his twin sister was holding his hand and thanking her brother for all she had learned from him. His closest friend and the hospice nurse, their arms around each other, softly prayed for him. No one was rushing around, lost in busyness and trying to avoid what had just happened. They were, in a very quiet and connected way, being with dying.

The practice of being with dying does not stop at the moment of death; as caregivers or family members who have been present at the death of a friend or relative, we may have the privilege of attending the body after death. Many of us today have lost a vital connection to the life cycle of birth and death, increasingly cut off as we are from traditional community and extended family. In previous centuries, it would have been unlikely that anyone would have reached adulthood without being present at the bedside of one or more deaths, and as a result our forebears might have had a healthier view of dying as the natural end to life. Instead, we're taught as small children to be frightened at the thought of a dead body, and we're often "protected" from, for example, the sight of a dead grandparent. The result is that most people are scared by the thought of a corpse, and we worry about whether we will be strong or brave enough to care for the empty vessel that once held a beloved friend or relative.

One simple but wise step that can help to prepare everyone is to initiate a conversation with the dying person about how she would like her body to be cared for. When David asked what would be done with his body immediately after he died, his question gave his family and friends the chance to sit with him and explore what he wanted and what might be possible. The frank conversation brought everyone closer to David and to the experience that was drawing nearer and nearer with every passing day.

If you're leading a group of caregivers, and if it's culturally and psychologically appropriate, you can help prepare friends and relatives for the moment of death by suggesting that they support an atmosphere of stillness and respect. Let them know what the moment of death might be like. Ultimately, it depends on how the person is dying, but often the actual moment of death is quite simple—just the long out-breath of release. Other deaths, as we've seen, are more strenuous, but inevitably the body will come to rest peacefully.

As caregivers, we need to be guided by the faith and beliefs of the dying person as we are present for them. Our challenge is to familiarize ourselves with the particulars of different faiths, and to encourage and be with whatever spiritual approaches are appropriate to a community and to the dying individual. That is why I often ask, "What guides and supports you in your life? What do you have faith in? What really matters to you?"

One caregiver shared with me how she assisted a death:

> I'm dismayed about how people often die in the hospital these days, without acknowledgment of the essential sacredness of this transition. We did the most beautiful thing on Friday. I was caring for a twenty-year-old Cambodian woman in a persistent vegetative state from an accident years ago. The family had blessedly decided to withdraw ventilator support and tube

feeds. I asked the father if they had a faith tradition. "Buddhist," he said. I asked if he would like me to arrange some prayers for his daughter and he said yes. I called the other nurse (who had just spent a week in solitary retreat, reading *The Tibetan Book of Living and Dying,* by Sogyal Rinpoche) and she did the most beautiful prayer service, singing and chanting the Heart Sutra and other prayers, sitting in silence as the girl's life ebbed. I put a mala around her head and taped pictures of buddhas around her hospital bed. The room filled with silence and peace.

Many traditions believe that the deceased's spirit or consciousness remains present for a time—maybe still in the body, maybe nearby. Caregivers want to show respect for this presence while still being in a practical relationship with the body, taking care of what needs to be done. And every culture has its own sacred methods for preparing a body for funeral, burial, or cremation. What follows are only some suggestions for how to be with this final aspect of dying.

Immediately following death, try to keep the atmosphere around the deceased simple and quiet. If possible, don't disturb or touch the body; if the body absolutely must be touched or moved, do so very gently. Everyone nearby can pray for peace and freedom for the one who has died. If appropriate, read sacred texts or conduct any practices or rituals from the deceased's tradition. Since rigor mortis takes about two hours to set in, you will have plenty of time to bathe and dress the body—there isn't any need to hurry, so don't rush anything.

Again and again I've witnessed it as deeply healing for family members or friends to bathe and prepare the body they loved, as a last act of intimacy and respect. Although nowadays we're often fearful of this task, and turn it over to the hospital or funeral home, we can really use this precious opportunity to help our community come together after the loss of a loved one.

Please be aware that just before and right at the moment of death, the dying person may have defecated, urinated, vomited, or sweated. Instead of using plain water, you may want to give the body a sponge bath with a mixture of alcohol (use just a small amount, to close the pores) and a mild aromatic tea (there are many herbal teas available).

If the deceased is going to "rest in state" at one's home, here are some other suggestions. Place cotton in the rectum so that wastes do not leak from the body, and either a condom on the penis or cotton in the vagina. If you like, clean the teeth and mouth. Don't remove dentures or you may not be able to put them back in after rigor mortis sets in. Sometimes, muscle spasms occur in the limbs or facial muscles after death; don't be concerned if this happens, as occasional reflexive movements are common.

Mindfully dress and arrange the body before it stiffens. Choose lightweight clothing, and don't cover the body with bedding. The body needs to stay as cool as possible. Use air conditioning, a fan, dry ice, or an open window to help keep the air fresh around the body.

Often, the eyes have remained open during and after death. If you wish, you can gently close the lids and tape them shut.

The mouth, too, might be open. You can close it with a scarf tied around the head. Since death reminds us of sleep, arranging the face in a peaceful expression of sleep can make the appearance of the deceased seem less strange to family and friends. After a short amount of time, the tape and scarf can be removed.

The body will gradually begin to cool as time passes; the last place in the body from which warmth will leave is the heart area. If warmth is still emanating from the heart, be particularly mindful of what is happening in the environment of the deceased. Buddhist tradition tells us that such warmth usually occurs in those who have some quality of realization at the time of death.

Although you might be concerned that it's unhealthy to keep a body in the house, even for a short while, there is nothing inherently dangerous about doing so. Simply treat a dead body in the same way you would a living one, following the same health precautions, particularly if the person died of a communicable disease.

In the United States a doctor needs to sign a death certificate. It is usually easiest to minister to the body before contacting the doctor about the death certificate. When you contact the crematorium or a burial society, members of its staff usually come to collect the body quite quickly. If you wish to let the body rest undisturbed, you might want to wait a while before you contact these organizations. Be sure to remove jewelry before the body goes to the funeral home; it can be placed on the body again later, if desired.

In most places in the United States, family members or religious groups are allowed to serve as funeral directors. If this is what you decide to do, you may need a permit to move the body yourself, and you will need to file the required burial or cremation document.

An unembalmed body should be buried or cremated within several days in order to prevent bacteria from multiplying to unhealthy levels. Contrary to what many morticians suggest, embalming is not required unless the body is being shipped out of state, although many states require that the body be refrigerated within twenty-four to forty-eight hours after death. Be aware that embalming does not sterilize the body. Actually, the chemicals used in the embalming process are toxic to the living and are regulated by the government as hazardous materials. If you plan to digress from a conventional burial, investigate the laws in your area beforehand, and don't depend on funeral homes or hospital staff to help you figure out alternatives to standard procedures.

Burial on your own property is permitted in many places in the United States. If home burial is chosen, keep in mind that future owners of the land may move the grave or may not permit visitors.

Cremation has become more common in recent years, and many dying people prefer it. When my father died, the National Cremation Society came for his body in our home. The last I ever saw of him was somewhat distressing, as I watched the gurney being pushed down the hallway onto an elevator, and then saw my father's body tipped onto its head just as the elevator door closed. The unusualness continued. My stepmother collected his ashes from the crematorium and refused to give them up for the memorial service. Finally, our lawyer called to remind her that anything that had belonged to my father before their marriage would go to his daughters—including his body. She relented, and we followed my father's wishes, scattering his and my mother's ashes in the Gulf of Mexico. This journey around my father's death was quite a humbling one for all of us. Often this is the case. The odd and wonderful, sad and distressing, happen around death. And so be it.

I've been asked many times, "What about organ donation?" Personally, I value both options—donation as a compassionate gift to the living and the option of not disturbing the body after death. Ultimately, it is a deeply personal choice for everyone. While it's often guided by social or cultural values, it's also important not to impose your own or your family's beliefs onto the dying person's wishes. If you can, ask the dying one what he would prefer, and then support his choice.

Jishu, who was a Buddhist priest, decided years ago that when she died, she wanted to donate her organs for the benefit of others. She was aware that in the Buddhist tradition, you don't disturb the body for several days, until its burial. But after she reflected, and asked other practitioners, she felt that the most compassionate thing to do was to benefit the lives of others. She's not alone—many Buddhists believe there is great merit in choosing to donate one's organs.

It turned out that due to her prior illnesses, Jishu could only donate her corneas. Since corneas can be harvested as late as several hours after death, we who loved her were given plenty of time to be with her body, and to offer gratitude for all that this woman had given, both to us and to many others.

Jishu had died suddenly at the age of fifty-seven after several heart attacks. Her death gave many of us the opportunity to express the inexpressible in the way we cared for her body. When Jishu's heart finally gave out in the hospital, her life support was disconnected; she slipped quietly into death. We asked the hospital staff in the coronary unit for their help, and they gave us warm water and cloths to bathe Jishu's face and neck. Then we sat with her and prayed.

Jishu's funeral was scheduled to take place a week after her death. On the evening before the funeral, the funeral home allowed us to take her body to the house where she and her husband had just moved—the new home she had enjoyed for only one week before her first heart attack.

That night, her mother, her husband, and her many women friends gathered around the bed where her body lay. We wanted to bathe and dress Jishu before the funeral and her "fire samadhi," or cremation. At first, Jishu's mother was very tentative and hesitant about being part of this, but finally she decided she would participate, and at least try to be with her daughter this way.

We began to bathe Jishu as a friend sang nearby. And then Jishu's mother reached through the throng of women surrounding her daughter's body and began to bathe her face lovingly. The rest of us bathed Jishu's body; then her mother combed and arranged her hair. We dressed her in Buddhist priest robes and wrapped her body in a quilt that her mother had made. For many of us who attended her funeral the next day, this was the strongest and most intimate moment.

The practice of bathing and caring for the dead is common the world over, and very often has a profound effect on the family and friends who participate in the ritual. We don't need to worry about whether we will be adequate to the task; caring for the empty vessel is just another facet of caregiving, and a very meaningful way to express how grateful we are to have been a part of this person's life—and death. Being with the body of a deceased person offers us a precious chance to make a whole cloth out of death and grieving, bringing the circle of being with dying to completion and healing.

## MEDITATION

### Charnel Ground Meditation

A traditional Tibetan saying tells us that if, on waking up in the morning, we do not meditate on death, the entire morning will be wasted. If we don't meditate on death at noon, the afternoon will be wasted. And if we don't meditate on death in the evening, the night will be lost to meaningless and frivolous pursuits.

The simple Buddhist practice that follows provides us with a graphic way to meditate on death. In it we visualize the decomposition of our body after death through nine stages of dissolution. The practice points us toward seeing the impermanent nature of this body and, by association, of all phenomena. It also reminds us of the emptiness of the self.

Traditionally one goes to a charnel ground to do this practice, directly observing bodies in various states of decomposition. In 1999, on the western side of Mount Kailash in Tibet, I had the opportunity to practice with human remains from two sky burials. Doing walking meditation among pools of blood, bones, and the two faces shorn of their skulls, their bloody hair in a tangled mess, I felt quite vigilant.

A Tibetan approached who "specialized" in the ritual of carving up dead people so that the vultures could more eadily consume the reamins. He invited me to lie among these fresh human remains. Lying in a pool of human blood and fat was a disturbing and vivid experience. He then took a knife out of a sheath beneath his coat and began to mime chopping up my body. For a moment I felt overwhelmed with disgust. Then suddenly I relaxed into the realization that I, too, am blood and fat. I began to let go of the wave of aversion washing over me and I gazed up at the mountain, remembering that sooner or later, I also will be dead. As the old man wielded his long, rusty knife above me, I visualized myself as a dead body.

Of course, you don't need to go to Tibet and offer yourself to such a wild moment. The practice outlined below is an extraordinary way for us to release our story into the liberating truth that we know as impermanence.

Let your body settle as you bring awareness to your breath. Recall your aspiration to free all beings from suffering. Rest in presence before you begin, following the breath.

Now imagine that you are observing your body as a corpse. You are sitting next to and observing this form that once was you. All is still. You have died this day.

Look closely. Notice the pallid face and sunken cheeks. The skin is smooth and waxy. Observe the shadowy mottling on the underside of the arms and legs. With no blood pressure, the blood is pooling. Observe the fingernails; they are pale and bloodless. In this stillness, the whole body appears to have sunk into itself. The skin is pale, with a gray-blue cast.

The eyelids seem almost transparent. The eyes are dry, opaque, and slightly open, gazing into nowhere. The mouth is slack, with the jaw dropped open.

Now imagine that several hours have passed. This body that once was you seems to have grown darker. Its shadowy color has deepened. There is now a slight odor to the body. Reach out to touch this body. Feel the cool and lifeless flesh. This body, which once was you, is now cold, stiff, dead weight.

Three days pass, and you are still sitting in front of the body. It is now bloated and festering, swollen with bacteria and gases. The smell coming from this body that once was you is strong and putrid.

Several more days pass. Still you are sitting in front of this body, looking closely at it. You see something move. Maggots are feeding off this body. Flies land on the body. Other insects are laying their eggs in this rotting body. The odor from the body is strong. Open yourself to the truth of the change in this body.

Two more days pass. Crows arrive and start pulling at the decaying flesh. Other carrion eaters rival one another to consume this rotting body. Flesh is torn from bone. Tissue is stripped from calf and thigh, from arms and chest. The belly is ripped open. More and more bones are exposed.

A month has passed since the time of death. You are still sitting in front of this body that once was you. All that is left now is a skeleton with some flesh on it. Look deeply. If this is all that it has come to, what was your life about? Just this skeleton, with a little sinew here and there. Old blood staining the bones. Observe this skeleton.

Three months later this skeleton has just a few tendons holding bones together. Look with equanimity at the body as it disappears. Just a few tendons hold together this collection of bones.

More time passes. The tendons loosen their hold on the bones themselves. The bones of the feet have gone one way, the bones of the hands another. The thighbone, pelvis, and spinal vertebrae are coming apart. The body you took such good care of is just bare bones scattered around. You spent so much effort tending it, and all that remains is disconnected bones.

Six months later, still sitting there. Now all you see is a pile of old bleached white bones. The bones are beginning to fragment and turn to dust.

A year later, still sitting beside that which was your body, you see a pile of old bones, hard to distinguish one from another. Some have been carried off by animals. Weathered by sun, wind, and rain, the bones that are left crumble when touched.

Two years later you are sitting where once this body was. There is nothing left but dust. Wind rises and blows here and there the dust of what was your body. Ask yourself, Who is this?

Rest in presence. Let yourself stay with this openness. Wake up into its spaciousness. Let your mind settle into this truth: Your body is always changing. One day it will be dust. Awaken to this reality.

Please ask, Who dies?

# 19

## River of Loss
### *The Plunge of Sorrow*

I N THE EIGHTEENTH century, the Japanese haiku master Issa lost his baby daughter. Struggling to come to grips with his loss, utterly devastated, he wrote:

> The world of dew
> is the world of dew.
> And yet, and yet—*

We can tell that Issa hasn't been released from anguish; he can't comprehend how his baby girl's life could be as fleeting as the tiny, perfect world in a drop of morning dew. Yet even in this poem, we can see his tightly closed hand beginning to open.

Just like Issa's daughter's life, even grief is transient, and eventually it can pass through us and leaves us wiser and humbler for it. Before this transformation, though, we must do the slow work of swimming through it. To deny the pain and longing we feel is to rob ourselves of the heavy stones that will eventually be the ballast for the two great accumulations

---

* Kobayashi Issa, in *The Essential Haiku,* translated and edited by Robert Hass (New York: Ecco Press, 1994), 191.

of wisdom and compassion. When we face the difficult gift of loss, the experience of grieving can be like swallowing bitter medicine. Our whole being seizes up, and then something settles deep into our bones that gives us strength.

Grief also often touches the one who is dying, who can mourn in antici-pation of death and the loss of a whole life. Caregivers, too, are often sad-dened by the loss of freedom and options of those who are ill, and the knowledge that death will rob them of a precious relationship. Then there is the taste of grief embedded in our culture, which is conditioned to pos-sess and not let go.

Sometimes it may seem that Buddhism fails to address grief, maybe looking on it as a weakness of character or a failure of practice, even though there exist many Buddhist teachings about the tender heart of compassion that makes deep grieving possible. My first teacher, Zen Master Seung Sahn used to tell a story in which long ago, in ancient Korea, a young monk hiked up to the mountain cave of a master, hoping to hear his leg-endary teachings on impermanence. But when the monk got there, he was shocked to see the great master sobbing over the dead body of a fawn.

The monk asked the master what had happened, and the master told him how hunters had killed the baby deer's mother. He had nursed the fawn, going down into town every day to beg for milk so he could feed it. When no one would give him milk for a mere animal, the master told people it was for his son—though in fact they found it an even more repel-lent idea that a celibate priest would have a baby! In spite of their disap-proval, some people grudgingly gave him milk; but finally the situation became too scandalous and no one would help him anymore. The mas-ter wandered everywhere, begging, but by the time he finally found some milk and returned to the cave, the fawn had died.

"You don't understand," the master told the student. "My mind and the fawn's mind are the same. It was very hungry. I want milk, I want milk. Now it is dead. Its mind is my mind. That's why I am weeping: I want milk."[*]

---

[*] Seung Sahn, *Dropping Ashes on the Buddha: The Teachings of Zen Master Seung Sahn* (New York: Grove Press, 1976), 62.

As in all good Zen stories, at that moment the monk got it: The master was a bodhisattva, an enlightened being who has so much compassion that he chooses to remain here in this difficult existence with the rest of us so that he can offer his help. And it's precisely the experience of grieving that opens up this kind of compassion in our lives, serving as a crucible of maturation, giving our practice depth and humility—and a new wisdom.

That anxious heaviness of mourning can be the heart adjusting to the new and terrible weight of the one who is dying or has died, passing from the outside world to inside our being. C. S. Lewis described the feelings rising up from this act of possession. Those feelings are wired into the body, he says: the yawning for more air, the unsettling in the stomach, the repeated swallowing of an unaccepted sorrow, all sensations associated with fear. In his book *A Grief Observed*, he said, "No one ever told me that grief was so much like fear."

In this experience of blunt immediacy, we learn that fear and suffering can't be transformed by someone else telling us how to do it. Perhaps those close to us can help us through shining light into the darkness of our suffering, shouting encouragement as we learn to swim in the black, rushing waters of sorrow. But we have to pull ourselves through these waters to the other shore.

Christine had uterine cancer. She called and asked me to meet with her and her husband. No real emergency, she said, but would I come? Sitting with these two, I saw that Christine seemed to have accepted her imminent death—it was her husband who carried the suffering. Wound like a tight spring, with deep lines of worry and fear creasing his pale brow, he was bubbling beneath the surface with anxious anger. I sat there with the two of them and listened as Christine helped Dan find his footing. Her words were like saving stones in the rough waters of anticipatory grief. And Christine was an iron woman as she laid down the stones for Dan to step on. She could not and would not walk those stones for him.

The sorrow of all our human losses, great and small, anticipatory or contemporary, feeds into a river that runs underground beneath our lives. When that dark water breaks through the surface, at first we feel totally alone. We may truly believe, "No one but me has ever felt this kind of pain." And that is half the truth, for grieving spreads across a landscape so vast and varied that we can only really discover it through our own intimate experience.

When my mother died, I received one of the hardest and most precious teachings of my entire life. I realized that I only had this one chance to grieve her death. I felt like I had a choice. On the one hand, I could be a so-called "good Buddhist," accept impermanence, and let go of my mother with great dignity. The other alternative was to scour my heart out with honest sorrow.

I chose to scour. After her death, I went to the desert with photographs of her and letters she had written my father after I was born. Settling under a rocky ledge, I sank back into shadows of sorrow. When your mother dies, so does the womb that gave birth to you. I felt that my back was uncovered and exposed even as I pressed it into cold, solid rock. Later, I walked the Himalayas with a friend who had recently lost his mother, too. The autumn rains washed down the mountains and streaked down our wet faces.

When my friend and I arrived in Kathmandu, the lamas there offered to perform a Tibetan ceremony for my mother. They instructed me not to cry but to let her be at peace. By this time, I felt ready to hear their words, and I did not have to force myself to stop mourning. When I let myself drop all the way through to the bottom, I found that my mother had become an ancestor. As I finally released her, she became part of me. And my sadness became part of the river of grief that pulses deep inside us, hidden from view but informing our lives at every turn.

Our struggles usually begin when we don't attend sufficiently to the painful, strong emotions that flood us just after the loss of a loved one. It's so easy for family and friends to let their feelings become consumed in the urgent "busyness of business" right after their loved one has died. In the West, business has unfortunately become an enormous part of the dying experience. The deceased's survivors face a complex material situation in the after-death phase. They find themselves looking for a funeral home, notifying friends and family, creating a funeral service, and unraveling health insurance, taxes, and the last will and testament. And then there's cleaning up, dividing and giving away the deceased's property. In the midst of the seemingly endless chores of closure, it's tempting for survivors to resort to the excuse of busyness to avoid the depth of their own loss: "I'll grieve later—right now I just don't have time."

At first, grief is overwhelming, whether you're anticipating the loss of your own life or living with the loss of another. We pass through the dark realms of the five elements of earth, water, fire, air, and space, each one part of the intensely physical experience of grieving. As we move through these elements and their terrible transformations, often feeling as forsaken as Christ in his final hours, it's normal to feel heavy with guilt or contracted in shame. We might find ourselves resenting the well-meaning friends who offer reassurances such as "This too shall pass"—this kind of comfort seems shallow and defensive, given the magnitude of our loss. But at the same time, we might still care what others think; we worry that we're trying the patience of our friends, or that we're an embarrassment to them with what seems like maudlin repetitiveness and self-pity.

But be aware that grief, like death, is natural. Even animals grieve. At a zoo in India some years ago, two female elephants were housed together. When one died in childbirth, the other, seventy-two years old, was inconsolable. She refused food and water, wept, and finally collapsed and died. As mammals, we form complex bonds with one another, and when these bonds are broken, our very bodies grieve.

Not getting thrown aside by shame, but staying present with sadness, is one way to give no fear to grief—just as the Buddha helped a woman drowning in grief over the death of her child by bringing her face-to-face with her sorrow. Ubbiri came from a very important family in India. Even when she was a little girl, she was incredibly beautiful, and when she grew up, she married a king. When Ubbiri gave birth to a daughter, she joyfully named her child Jiva, which means "alive." But not very long after being born, Jiva suddenly died.

Ubbiri was devastated by her grief, torn and wounded. She went every day to the cremation ground to mourn her daughter. One day when she got there, a great crowd had gathered: the Buddha, who was traveling through the region, had stopped to offer teachings to the local people. Ubbiri listened to the Buddha for a while, but then left to go to the riverside, as usual, where she wept with despair. The Buddha heard her pain-filled keening. He sought her out and asked why she was weeping. In agony she cried out that her daughter was dead. He then pointed to first one place and then another where the dead had lain, and said to her:

> Mother, you cry out "O Jiva" in the woods.
> Come to yourself, Ubbiri.
> Eighty-four thousand daughters
> all with the name "Jiva"
> have burned in the funeral fire.
> For which one do you grieve?*

Notice that the Buddha isn't telling Ubbiri not to grieve. He's gently tugging open her individual grief into the wider possibility of universal compassion. The Buddha is pointing her toward the place where personal loss is transformed into a piercing tenderness toward everyone who's ever suffered—*all* of the eighty-four thousand mothers; all of the mothers who ever lived, including herself. And she needs the awareness of a greater community in order to recover and heal fully.

Grief is like the mother I heard about who bathed her dead baby in her own breast milk. She teaches us tenderness and patience with our own sorrow, and reminds us lovingly not to hold on too tightly. Impermanence is inescapable, we learn; no one and nothing escapes her touch.

---

* Susan Murcott, *First Buddhist Women: Poems and Stories of Awakening* (Berkeley, Calif.: Parallax Press, 2006), 94.

# MEDITATION

## *Encountering Grief*

The following practices, based on the boundless abodes, are phrases that guide us again and again into the deep waters of grief. Transformation may come when we are touched by loss, come to know it, and experience purification through being fully washed in its waters.

When practicing these phrases, let the body settle; you can either sit or lie down. Remember why you are practicing; cultivate a tender heart. Then find the phrase or phrases appropriate to you and practice them with the breath, or let your attention be gently with each phrase as you work with it.

- May I be open to the pain of grief.
- May I find the inner resources to be present for my sorrow.
- May I accept my sadness, knowing I am not my sadness.
- May I accept my anger, fear, anxiety, and sorrow.
- May I accept my grief, knowing that it does not make me bad or wrong.
- May I forgive myself for not meeting my loved one's needs.
- May I forgive myself for mistakes made and things left undone.
- May I be open with myself and others about my experience of suffering and loss.
- May I find peace and strength that I may use my resources to help others.
- May all those who grieve be released from their sorrow.

Life and death are of supreme importance.
Time passes swiftly and opportunity is lost.
Let us awaken
      awaken. . . .
Do not squander your life.

*Zen Night Chant*

# Afterword

## *Being One with Dying: Showing Up for the Great Matter*

THORNTON WILDER'S famous novel *The Bridge of San Luis Rey* imagines the lives of five people killed in the collapse of a bridge in Peru. In the novel, a missionary watches the falling bridge "fling five gesticulating ants into the valley below." Curious, he sets out to trace the lives of the victims in an effort to understand the seemingly random nature of the tragedy.

Really, Wilder's story is a parable of the struggle to find meaning in chance and in inexplicable tragedy—a struggle the victims' relatives face after the disaster. Wilder explained that he himself was seeking the answer to a question: "Is there a direction and meaning in life, beyond the individual's own will?"*

His story reminds us that death isn't only for the dying—it is also for those who survive us. Indeed, dying is not an individual act. A dying person is often a performer in a communal drama. Like our last will and testament, a legacy that materially benefits our survivors, we also leave a legacy of how we experience our death. And the bulk of that legacy comes from how we transition through the ultimate rite of passage—how we are able to be with our own dying.

---

* Thornton Wilder, *The Bridge of San Luis Rey* (New York: HarperCollins, 2004), 107.

Often we take part in rites of passage without being aware of what we are doing, or without having the transition and its shifts in consciousness acknowledged by our culture. Long, sleepless hours, high pressure, and the presence of suffering, death, and the mysterious unknown are ingredients in such rites.

Even though we may not call them rites of passage, such universal transitions in everyone's life include the elements of separation, the threshold, and return. Often we are not fully present for these experiences, the tide's deep ebb, because they may be painful or frightening. They include being ill and recovering our health, making love for the first time, giving birth to a child. And dying is possibly the ultimate example of such a transition. Death urges us to accept and appreciate our lives, to forgive ourselves and others, and to let go as the small self is dissolved into a larger stream of being. From the perspective of Buddhism, this is the greatest opportunity for awakening and freedom—as Emerson said, the wounded oyster that mends itself with a pearl.

But what rituals do we have in our culture that denote and legitimize such transformative passages? Practically none. Our society does not view catastrophe as a passage. Instead, chaotic, frightening experiences are usually controlled and suppressed. They aren't conditions with which our society is comfortable.

Yet even without support we instinctively seek the experience of separation, the threshold or being on the edge, and return. Clearly, dying and death in our culture are a rite of passage, whether we realize it or not. Some people experience a mental breakdown that induces maturity. Others, suffering, resolve to enter a strong spiritual practice. Some become physically ill and then evolve into wounded healers, turning outward to help others after having healed themselves. And of course, many people in their experience of dying "unconceal" their own natural wisdom. My father became even wiser as he was dying. Issan Dorsey became a true Zen man as he died. My friend Julie matured into a teacher as she lay dying. And Ann, the brilliant physician and research scientist, found faith beyond language as her brain was taken over by an aggressive death-dealing tumor.

Strange to say, but catastrophe is usually the circumstance that liberates strength, wisdom, and kindness from within the suffocating embrace of fear. Dying, we can be more alive. Being present and giving care in the midst of a meltdown of mind or life can seed compassion. This is how we mature, and how transparency and intimacy are engendered. Our very physical and psychic vulnerability, if we allow it, shows us the path and the present. It can also nurture gratitude and humility. Catastrophe is the essence of the spiritual path, a series of breakdowns allowing us to discover the threads that weave all of life into a whole cloth.

Years ago, when I visited Biosphere 2 in Arizona, I asked the scientist taking me around why there were wires tied to the trees and attached to the Biosphere's frame high above us. He explained that since there was no wind in the Biosphere, the trees had nothing to resist. As a result, they had grown weak and needed to be held up. Like our body and bones, we need something against which to resist in order to make us stronger.

How, then, I have asked myself over the years, can we truly be with dying, this invisible road of initiation that will open for all of us? How can we let it tear us apart and, by so doing, strengthen us? For me, living with the three tenets of not-knowing, bearing witness, and compassionate action has been like having a key that opens many doors, doors that have led to the same place—the unknown, the inconceivable, the place of simply being present for the truth of what is happening. Over time the tenets have sunk like sweet water into the ground of my daily life, including my work with dying people. I have come to see the tenets as a boat that takes me across uncharted waters. I turn my mind and heart to them in order to remind me of what I hope to realize in my interactions with those who are dying.

These tenets help me remember with some humility how I can be more intimate with and transparent to whatever is unfolding in the present moment. They help me act more skillfully as I spend time with those who are suffering. They guide me toward inclusiveness, and toward the contemplative practices that are the heart and bone of being with dying. Mindful contemplation deepens our capacity for concentration, openness, and insight, so that we gradually expand the horizons of our hearts until they are big enough to include everything, including the reality of death and the fact that even when someone dies "well," it may not be a pretty picture.

Giving care to a dying person and his or her family is an extraordinary practice that puts one in the midst of the unknowable, the unpredictable, the breakdown of life; it is often something that we have to push against. Physical illness, weakness of mind and body, being in the crosshairs of the medical establishment, and losing all that the dying person has worked to accumulate and preserve can be the hard and pulling tide of dying. A caregiver can be there for all of that, plus the miracles and surprises of the human spirit. And she can learn and even be strengthened at every turn. This is a real path of discovery when we let go into it as we give care. Whether family or professional, caregivers walk a path that is traceless, humbling, and often full of awe. And like it or not, most of us will find ourselves on it. We will accompany loved ones and others as they die.

If we are fortunate, we will be there for our own death as well. A dying person can meet the precious companions of truth, faith, and surrender. He or she can be entered by grace and space like a river flowing into the ocean or clouds disappearing into the sky.

For practicing dying is also practicing living, if we can only realize it. The more truly we can see this, the better we can serve those who are actively dying and offer them our love without condition.

Thornton Wilder's novel concludes:

> But soon we shall die and all memory of those five will have left earth, and we ourselves shall be loved for a while and forgotten. But the love will have been enough.

Love was also the message from Martin Toler, a man who died several years ago, along with many other miners, in the Sago coal mine accident in West Virginia. Slowly dying in the thickening air of the mine shaft, the oxygen wicked up with every breath, Toler used what precious little energy he had left in his life to write a note of reassurance to those closest to him—as well as to the millions of us who later heard about it.

From deep inside the earth, Toler addressed the entire world, beginning his note, "Tell all, I see them on the other side." He promises his kin to meet them in eternal life—in the place that is deathless. He expresses for all of us the deep human wish that our connections will transcend the event of separation we suffer at the moment of death. "It wasn't bad, just went to sleep," the note continues, and scrawled at the bottom, with the last of his ebbing strength, the tender, unselfish words "I love you."

I have often sat by the bedside of dying people with their relatives close at hand, waiting for those last words of love and hope. Being on the threshold between life and death gives an aura of mystery and truth to the final utterances of the dying. We who wait feel we can somehow penetrate the thin veil between the worlds through the words of the dying one; those so close to death might know what we all long to know.

Toler's last words honor the noblest in our human connections, that life is sacred and relationship holy. Through the darkness, he reached out not only to his family but to the rest of us, including us in his community through his abiding and compassionate words. For, as the Buddha told his cousin Ananda, the whole of the holy life is good friends. Our relationships—and our love—are ultimately what give depth and meaning to our lives.

What message do we want to leave behind when we die? When poet Elizabeth Barrett Browning died, she uttered one word: "Beautiful." "I am not in the least afraid to die!" exclaimed scientist Charles Darwin. And Thomas Edison, the genius inventor, said only, "It is very beautiful over there." These wise people on the threshold of death carry a message to the rest of us that death is our friend and not to be feared. What have they seen that we wish we could know? What is this mystery that all of us will enter?

All of these last words are deep teachings about how we can commend our spirit to the experience of dying—and how we may live in the meantime. They are a treasured testament of the human heart that calls us to transcend suffering and find redemption by encountering death fearlessly and even beautifully. Thus we come to understand directly the truth of impermanence, the intense fragility of all that we love, and that, in the end, we can really possess nothing. Yes, we may meet each other on "the other side." Yet we may also ask ourselves, Can we meet ourselves and each other now? Knowing that death is inevitable, what is most precious to us today?

We cannot know death, except by dying. This is the mystery that lies beneath the skin of life. But we can feel something from those who are close to it. Martin Toler said, "I love you." He said, in effect, everything is OK. In being with dying, we arrive at the natural crucible of what it means to love and be loved. In this burning fire we test our practices of not-knowing, bearing witness, and compassionate action, practices that can also hold us up through the most intense flames. Please, let us not lose our precious opportunity to show up for this great matter—indeed, the *only* matter—the awesome matter of life and death.

# Acknowledgments

I HAVE MANY people to thank for making this book possible. For those who have taught me through their grieving, sickness, and dying, I need to express my tender respect. For those who gave me refuge and support over these many years of sitting with dying people and teaching caregivers, my greatest gratitude: Tony Back, Roshi Richard Baker, Irène Kyojo Bakker, Sarah Barber, Mary Catherine Bateson, Gregory Bateson, Jonathon Berg, Richard Boestler, Dale Borglum, Ira Byock, Joseph Campbell, Annette Cantor, David Cantor, Venerable Chagdud Tulku Rinpoche, David Chambers, Sandy Chan, Gigi Coyle, Grant Couch, His Holiness the Dalai Lama, Ram Dass, Joe David, Lisl Dennis, Larry and Barbara Dossey, Ann Down, Scott Eberle, Katherine Foley, Jane Fonda, Verona, Dana, and John Fonte, Steven Foster, Ghelek Rinpoche, Roshi Bernie Glassman, Natalie Goldberg, Joseph Goldstein, Sallie Goodman, Rose Gordon, Jonna Goulding, Fleur Green, Christie Greene, Stanislav Grof, Lama Gyaltrul Tulku Rinpoche, Bessie Bandy Halifax, John and Eunice Halifax, Larry Hall, Charles and Susan Halpern, Francis Harwood, Ted Heffernan, Michael Henry, Barry Hershey, Roshi Jishu Angyo Holmes, Allan and Marion Hunt-Badiner, Edwin and Adrienne Joseph, Jon Kabat-Zinn, John and Tussi Kluge, Elizabeth Kübler-Ross, Andrea Kydd, Rob Lehman, Stephen Levine, Meredith Little, Alan Lomax, Christine Longacre, Fleet Maull, Patrick McNamara, Margaret Mead,

Dick Miller, Thich Nhat Hanh, Lukas Niederberger, Mayumi Oda, Roshi Enkyo O'Hara, Frank Ostaseski, Susan and George Otero, Manny Papper, Gary Pasternak, Marty Peale, Louise Pearson, Kathleen Priest, Ram Dass, Annie Rafter, Laurance Rockefeller, Gisela Roessiger, Larry Rosenberg, Cynda Rushton, John Russell, Sharon Salzberg, Dame Cecily Saunders, Seung Sahn Dae Soen Sa Nim, Diane Shainberg, Patricia Shelton, Larry Sherwitz, Huston Smith, Beverly Spring, Brother David Steindl-Rast, Gwynn Sullivan, Sensei Kazuaki Tanahashi, Elizabeth Targ, Tempa Dukte Lama, Chögyam Trungpa Rinpoche, the Sangha of Upaya Zen Center, Andy Weill, Jean Wilkins, Jack Zimmerman, and Zuleikha.

I want to offer gratitude to Emily Sell, Emily Bower, and Peter Turner at Shambhala for their great support and patience. And a special thanks to Jennifer Lowe, who worked with the final version of the book, bringing it home.